Biological Anthropology:
An Evolutionary Perspective
Part II

Professor Barbara J. King

THE TEACHING COMPANY ®

PUBLISHED BY:

THE TEACHING COMPANY
4840 Westfields Boulevard, Suite 500
Chantilly, Virginia 20151-2299
1-800-TEACH-12
Fax—703-378-3819
www.teach12.com

ISBN 1-56585-826-3

Barbara J. King, Ph.D.

Professor of Anthropology, The College of William and Mary

Barbara J. King, a biological anthropologist, specializes in the study of primate behavior and human evolution. Since 1988, she has taught at The College of William and Mary and has won four teaching awards: the William and Mary Alumni Association Teaching Award, the College's Thomas Jefferson Teaching Award, the Virginia State Council of Higher Education's Outstanding Faculty Award, and the designation of University Professor for Teaching Excellence, 1999–2002.

Professor King's research interests center around the social communication of the great apes, the closest living relatives to humans. Currently, she and her students observe and film the gestural communication of gorillas living at the Smithsonian's National Zoological Park, in Washington, D.C. Funded by the Wenner-Gren Foundation for Anthropological Research, this research is the basis of her new book. Tentatively titled *The Dynamic Dance: Nonvocal Social Communication in the Great Apes*, this book will be completed during Professor King's year as a Guggenheim Foundation Fellow (academic year 2002–2003).

Other books authored or co-authored by Professor King reflect her longstanding interest in the "big issues" in anthropology. One such book, *The Information Continuum* (1994), is based on her doctoral research into baboon social learning in Kenya, and two others, edited volumes, resulted from major funded conferences in anthropology (*The Origins of Language*, 1999, and *Anthropology Beyond Culture*, co-edited with Richard Fox, 2002).

Professor King received her B.A. in anthropology from Douglass College, Rutgers University, and earned both her M.A. and Ph.D. in anthropology from the University of Oklahoma. At The College of William and Mary, she focuses on teaching primate studies and human evolution to undergraduates.

Professor King welcomes questions or comments at either of these addresses: Department of Anthropology, The College of William and Mary, Williamsburg, VA 23187-8795, or bjking@wm.edu.

Table of Contents
Biological Anthropology:
An Evolutionary Perspective
Part II

Acknowledgment:
Footage of a rhesus monkey on Cayo Santiago provided by Christy Hoffman.

Biological Anthropology:
An Evolutionary Perspective

Scope:

These 24 lectures present detailed, up-to-date material about all aspects of the evolution of humanity. Aimed at those who are curious about our origins as a species, this course covers the wide range of topics in the discipline of biological anthropology. Biological anthropology takes as its goal a comprehensive exploration of the forces of both biology and culture that shaped human prehistory and continue to shape our lives today.

Following an introductory explanation of the various scientific approaches that together make up the field of biological anthropology, the initial lectures focus on evolution and its mechanisms. Important concepts, such as Darwin's principle of natural selection, are defined clearly, with real-life examples, and their significance is explained. What emerges from this section of the course is an understanding of why evolution and religious faith never need be opposed, whereas evolution and the theory of creationism are in direct conflict (with creationism rejected by scientists).

Applying these concepts to evolutionary history, Lectures Four through Eight explore the origins and behavior of the nonhuman primates. As primates ourselves, we humans share a 65-million-year evolutionary history with prosimians, monkeys, and apes. These lectures concentrate on primate behavior, showing how our own cognition, language, and kinship bonds developed out of the abilities present in these primate relatives. Particular emphasis is put on the great apes, such as chimpanzees, those animals closer to us genetically and behaviorally than any other.

The hominids, our extinct ancestors that walked upright, evolved from a common ancestor with the great apes nearly 7 million years ago. The anatomy and behavior of these species, ranging from the famous "Lucy," to the less well-known but equally important "Nariokotome Boy," to the cave-dwelling Neandertals, are profiled in Lectures Nine through Fifteen. These lectures highlight ways in which biology and culture intersect to allow for milestones to be reached in human prehistory.

Examples include the enlarged brain that allowed stone tools to be manufactured for the first time by hominids at 2.5 million years ago and the increasing cognitive skills and emotional ties that together led to deliberate burial of the dead by Neandertals at about 60,000 years ago. Two lectures deal with issues related to gender in prehistory, asking what we can know about the relative roles of females and males in hominid societies.

Lectures Sixteen through Eighteen are devoted to the origins of modern human anatomy, behavior, and language. Biological anthropologists have identified what they believe to be the oldest modern-human remains at about 125,000 years ago. For reasons made clear, it is unlikely that these earliest *Homo sapiens* could have evolved from Neandertals. From which hominids, then, did they arise? Was Africa the center of modern human origins, as it had been the center for early hominid evolution? We consider two competing models in evaluating these questions. One model points to Africa as the sole home of our species, whereas the other posits simultaneous evolution in Africa, Asia, and Europe.

Even more debated are the origins of modern human behavior and language. New evidence points to significant shifts in biological anthropologists' understanding of each of these topics. Sites in Africa tell us that symbolism, art, and finely crafted tools may not have first appeared at 35,000 years ago in Europe as long thought; evidence for a long evolutionary history for language is mounting as well.

The final five lectures consider modern human life in evolutionary perspective. A near-consensus conclusion in biological anthropology, that the practice of grouping humans into "races" based on supposedly genetic traits is invalid scientifically, forms the heart of Lecture Nineteen. Subsequent lectures explore ways in which evolution has tailored human anatomy and behavior, even today, to specific environmental pressures.

Also considered at length are fascinating new suggestions that modern health problems and aspects of modern health psychology have arisen as a direct result of conditions in human prehistory—conditions to which we were once adapted but no longer are. Pregnancy sickness and human mate choice are two case studies in this section.

The course concludes with a look at 21st century "gene discourse," in which undue power is given to genes and genetic research as panaceas for the future. An evolutionary perspective yields an understanding that the kinship we humans feel with other primate species (both living and extinct), as well as the tools we collectively have at our disposal for solving conflicts and other problems, are based not on genetics. Rather, they stem from a dynamic interplay of biological and cultural factors at work in our long evolutionary history.

Lecture Thirteen
Who Were the Neandertals?

Scope:

No hominids pique greater interest, or are more shrouded in mystery, than the Neandertals. Did the Neandertals resemble the shambling cavedwellers so beloved by fiction writers, B-movie makers, and cartoonists? Or were they, in fact, relatively advanced, well-adapted primates, more like humans in many ways than like early hominids?

Biological anthropologists favor the second view. Neandertals were large-brained, bipedal walkers. Neandertals were significantly more stocky and muscled than are modern humans, however, with a very differently shaped skull.

Neandertal behavior is by no means primitive. These hominids made significant technological advances, hunted big game successfully, and even buried their dead—an act not associated with *Homo erectus*. The latest anthropological interpretations emphasize these advances while noting that bands of Neandertals were likely not as efficient in survival skills as were groups of modern humans.

As we will see, no consensus exists about the precise nature of the relatedness either between Neandertals and modern humans or among the other hominid species at this general time period. The interval between the latter *Homo erectus* time period and the disappearance of the Neandertals at approximately 30,000 years ago is currently a challenging one in paleoanthropology.

Outline

I. The Neandertals have been known to science since 1856 and, in that century and a half, have become a kind of cultural icon.

  A. Say "Neandertal," and the image that pops into many people's minds is that of an ancient, stooped, and not-so-clever "caveman" wearing animal skins. Asserting that someone today "thinks like a Neandertal" is far from a compliment.

  B. Historically, we can explain the source of this image. In 1911, a French anatomist reconstructed a Neandertal skeleton to represent just such a shambling, unintelligent creature.

1. The anatomist, like most others of his day, had a preconceived notion of what "ancient man" should look and act like.

2. He chose for reconstruction a skeleton whose bones were affected by arthritis, thus strengthening his conclusion that this hominid was far from modern in appearance.

II. Biological anthropologists now reject the "stooped caveman" reconstruction of Neandertals. Like other hominids, Neandertals were bipedal and show a mix of both more and less humanlike traits.

A. Neandertals were large-brained hominids and walked bipedally with a modern gait.

B. Neandertals were short, stocky, and extremely strong. This is one way in which they were markedly different in appearance from modern humans.

C. From the neck up, Neandertals, despite their large brains, had a more primitive look than do modern humans. The Neandertal skull, with its low forehead, large brow ridges, and enlarged nasal area, is distinctive.

III. The best way to think of the Neandertals is as an archaic species closely related to modern humans but different enough to be classified in its own species, *Homo neandertalensis*.

A. Precursors to Neandertal features can be traced in fossils as far back as 300,000 years ago.

B. Most biological anthropologists refer to Neandertals as living between 130,000 to 30,000 years ago, with emphasis on the period of the last glaciation, starting at 75,000 years ago. Neandertals lived in Europe and Asia.

C. Neandertals are different enough from *Homo sapiens* to warrant their own species. As we will see later, the two species did overlap in time and space.

IV. Behavior and culture of the Neandertals give intriguing hints that Neandertals were, in fact, complex thinkers. Biological anthropologists, however, disagree on how like modern humans they were in this regard.

A. The trend toward improved hominid technology over time continues with the Neandertals. Neandertal tools are based on flake manufacture.

B. Neandertals did sometimes live in caves and were successful hunters, proving that even oversimplified stereotypes do contain some truth! Some biological anthropologists suggest that their foraging patterns were more restricted and simplified than those of modern humans.

C. The area of interpretation about Neandertals that is subject to the most contention involves their cultural behavior.

    1. Deliberate burial of the dead by Neandertals is accepted by most scholars. Burials at a cave in Shanidar, Iraq, offer a good case study. Do these and other Neandertal burials involve some kind of symbolism? Here, little agreement exists.

    2. Can we find glimmers of early art among Neandertals? Biological anthropologists are skeptical.

V. The precise relationship of Neandertals to modern humans, and to other hominids of the same general time period, is unclear.

A. In these lectures, Neandertals are considered to belong to a separate species than modern humans. The Jurmain textbook recommended for this course, however, concludes that Neandertals are an archaic variant of our own species.

B. Analysis of ancient DNA may eventually reconcile this issue. At present, DNA analysis tends to support the view that Neandertals were a distinct species, but uncertainties surround this technique.

C. The time period directly before Neandertals appeared, that is, between 400,000 and 130,000 years ago, is best thought of as a transitional one. Several types of hominids may be present. Scientists are at work attempting to clarify the relationship of these species to both the earlier *Homo erectus* and the latter *Homo sapiens*.

D. In sum, Neandertal anatomy has come clearly into focus in recent decades, and we learn more about Neandertal behavior by the year. Yet the ancestral relationships among Neandertals, modern humans, and other hominids in this general time period remain fuzzy.

Essential Reading:

Jurmain et al., *Introduction to Physical Anthropology*, chapter 12.

Tattersall, *The Last Neanderthal*.

Questions to Consider:

1. State some significant ways in which Neandertals differ from *Homo erectus*. Consider both anatomy and behavior.

2. What are three possible interpretations for why Neandertals deliberately buried their dead? Are some of these interpretations more cognitively impressive than others?

Lecture Thirteen—Transcript
Who Were the Neandertals?

Welcome to a lecture that I expect will be fun, because in it we are going to confront the Neandertals, a hominid that I think is behaviorally quite compelling, and I might even say, enigmatic. I should say right at the outset that there's an alternative pronunciation or spelling of "Neanderthal" with a *th*, but "Neandertal" is more accurate, so that is the term we are going to use.

In this lecture we will also widen our focus geographically, and we'll begin to consider hominid occupation of a third continent, because we find Neandertals in Europe. They are, therefore, in Europe and Asia. We've been talking about Africa, but we won't in this lecture because Neandertals are not found in Africa.

Neandertals have been known to science since 1856. That's quite a long time. That's almost 75 years longer than we've known about the australopithecines, since Dart's discovery, and about 35 years longer than we've known about *Homo erectus*, since the time period of Dubois's discovery.

In that time, Neandertals have become something of a cultural icon. You say the term "Neandertal," and something usually comes to mind. A particular image usually comes to mind, and it's an interesting fact that this long period during which science has known about Neandertals has not really translated to accuracy of the images that tend to come to mind. Most people think about an ancient, stooped cave dweller, possibly somebody wearing animal hides, and grunting, and hunting mammoths. If you assert that someone else thinks like a Neandertal, this is most assuredly not a compliment.

I tell my students—especially in election years—when they're reading the newspaper, to read letters to the editor. Every now and then you'll be sure to come across one that accuses a politician or someone else of thinking like a Neandertal, and that is a code for thinking in a primitive and backwards type of way.

None of this image, the physical or the mental, is particularly accurate. Why did it arise then? Historically, we can explain the origins of this shambling, not-so-smart Neandertal. It goes back to 1911, which is the year in which a French anatomist decided to reconstruct a Neandertal from bones that had been dug up in his home country. These bones were found at the site of La Chapelle in

France. They were from a male who had died at about the age of forty.

The anatomist, Macellin Boule, constructed a human being—or almost human being—who looked very primitive. A shambling kind of bent-knee gait was assigned to this creature, and a kind of unintelligent look. Most important, perhaps, is the lack of full bipedalism that was put forth in this reconstruction. The textbook that I have recommended for this course describes the reconstruction as looking "bent-kneed and brutish," and that is a very good description of it, but we know from all the work that's gone on since that this is really quite inaccurate.

So let's push the question back one step further. If Boule was such an expert in anatomy, why did he make these mistakes? We will soon see that Neandertals were bipedal in the normal, modern way, and that they were not at all stupid. Boule, like others of his day, had certain preconceived notions of what an ancient man, so to speak, should look like. They should not look modern at all. They should be quite primitive.

In fact, by choosing to reconstruct the bones from La Chapelle, Boule had chosen a particularly robust specimen, not a very modern specimen in the array of Neandertal bones. But even more than that, no matter what bones he had chosen, he would have assumed that they should look non-modern. Furthermore, there was an additional factor. He selected a skeleton whose individual had suffered in life from osteoarthritis.

We know now that quite a few Neandertal skeletons show signs of arthritis, and this can distort and twist the bones. When he reconstructed this individual then, and did not realize that he was looking at arthritic bones, this factor only strengthened his conclusion of a brutish look. So clearly, his preconceptions overrode his anatomical expertise in this particular instance, and his reconstruction affected science and scientific models for many years; and continues, as I've hinted, to affect popular images of Neandertals.

Biological anthropologists very much reject the stooped caveman image of Neandertals. Like all the other hominids that we've been talking about, Neandertals did not have bent knees—they were bipedal—but they show a mix of more humanlike and less humanlike traits; and within Neandertals, there's also a range of variation. Those that are found in Western Europe—for example, in France—do tend to look more primitive and less modern. But let's look, as we usually do, at the pattern of Neandertal anatomy and not worry so much about all the exceptions.

Neandertals were large-brained hominids. It's kind of ironic that, in fact, we have discovered that their brains were, on average, larger than modern human brains—not by a lot, but by some. However, this does not mean that they really looked like us. They didn't. They were particularly robust, strong, short and squat, so their whole body plan and body shape was quite different.

The strength that this implies in their body deserves particular emphasis. We know from the enlarged joints, and the muscles that would have attached at those joints, that Neandertals, both men and women, would have been quite spectacularly strong compared to modern humans. So they had a body plan that was short and relatively squat.

You can think of this as the opposite of what we had talked about in the *Homo erectus* lecture. Back then, we talked about the Nariokotome Boy being hypertropically adapted: long body and long, slender limbs for heat dissipation. It's quite the opposite for Neandertals. They tend to live in cold areas and were *cold-adapted*, so the strength in the body plan seems to be a kind of response, an adaptive response, to a harsh life, and also a fairly cold life.

What about from the neck up? We've already talked about the large brain, but Neandertal skulls look entirely different than modern human skulls. For one thing, their forehead shows a very low brow. There's no high-domed forehead that we have. Brow ridges are quite prominent, these ridges of bone over the eye.

Also, the mid-facial region, particularly around the nose, is kind of pulled forward and elongated or enlarged, so there's a very particular Neandertal look with this enlarged nasal area. The front teeth tend to be quite big, as well—the incisors, the teeth that are in the front. So they are more modern post-cranially—below the neck—than they are cranially, although we have to factor in this strength differential that we had talked about already.

The best way to think of the Neandertals is as an ancient species that is not part of our species. In other words, the decision that I have made—and I'll talk about this again in a minute—is to go along with those biological anthropologists who classify Neandertals into their own species, *Homo neandertalensis.* This is very much staking a position, because it is part of a controversy, and not everybody agrees with this, but what we want to do is kind of set a foundation for how we're thinking of Neandertals, when and where they lived, so we will call them *Homo neandertalensis.*

We know that there are what we might call precursors of these Neandertal features that I've described for you visible in the archaeological record back to about 300,000 years ago, so there is a long lineage of individuals leading up to Neandertals. But by convention, we tend to refer to Neandertals proper as those individuals, like the ones I've described, living between 130,000 years ago and right around 32- or 30,000 years ago.

We know the most about Neandertals that lived from between about 75,000 years ago and about 32,000 years ago. That happens to coincide with a time period of the last glaciation of the Ice Age, and we have more information about that time period than about any other, but the key date to remember is the starting point at 130,000 years ago.

I've already mentioned the two continents on which Neandertals lived: Europe and Asia. We've also made mention of France and Germany as particular countries in which they were found. We could also mention some other examples of countries in which they've been found: Croatia, Israel and Iraq.

We want to focus a lot on their behavior, because this is where things get particularly interesting. There's a very hot debate about how much like modern humans were Neandertals in their behavior and in their cultural adaptations. We have intriguing hints that Neandertals were complex thinkers, but the question is, just how complex were they thinking? Were they thinking symbolically? How do we know? Here is where the disagreement lies.

So let's begin to assess some of what we do know about Neandertal behavior in both Europe and in Asia. The best place to start is probably the most concrete type of evidence, which is the technological material, the stone tools. We see that there has been technological advance with the Neandertals compared to all earlier hominids, so the trend that we have already noted towards improved stone tool technology over time just continues here with this hominid. Neandertal tools are based on flake manufacture.

You might say immediately, "Wait a minute. Didn't you earlier say that the Oldowan tools of *Homo habilis* really seem to be focused on those small flakes that were struck off, and didn't we think that *Homo erectus* tools also involved a lot of flaking?" Yes, but the Neandertal tools are different, and here's how. The core, the piece of rock, the chert of the cores, was taken, and flakes were sliced off incrementally until the core was essentially used up. There might be a little bit left at the end. If there were, that would be discarded. In other words, we can think of this almost as an assembly line type of manufacture of tools, slicing off lots of flakes, and this is a very efficient, pound for pound, use of stone compared to what we had been talking about before.

When the flakes were then cut off of the core, they were what we call "retouched," or trimmed into different tools. So the flakes were made into different shapes and different size tools to form a proper toolkit. There were knives and all kinds of other tools that would be fashioned after the initial process of trimming. Biological anthropologists have been impressed not only with the range of tools that exist but also with the efficiency in the tool-making process that we can see from the actual remains.

Of course, there is some truth sometimes to popular images, and there is at least a bit of genuine information reflected in the image that we have of Neandertals as cave dwellers, because often they did live in caves. Sometimes they also lived in open areas though, and we have some intriguing evidence from the country of Moldova to show that this was so.

There is a ring of mammoth bones that are set up on an open plane, and in the middle of this ring there is a hearth, Neandertal tools, and animal bones. The hearth is a very good indicator of Neandertal control of fire. This is pretty unambiguous. What we imagine is that the ring of mammoth bones had skins stretched over them, animal hides stretched over them, so that this was a shelter. So we know that caves weren't the only places that Neandertals occupied, and there's a real search for finding other shelters as well, and some others have been found.

It's interesting that also, Neandertals were good hunters. This is another part of the stereotype that holds true. This is not to say that they were necessarily as efficient as modern humans, as *Homo sapiens*. For example, as far as we know, Neandertals did not have projectiles, weapons that would have allowed them to hunt from a distance. There's no example of a spear-thrower. There's no example of a bow and arrow. These enter the archaeological record only with modern humans, but yet they were successful at hunting, and we know this from various sites across Europe and Asia.

We also know this from a different source of information, as well. The biological anthropologist whom I consider to be the foremost Neandertal expert, Eric Trinkaus, has studied the diet of Neandertals in various ways, including chemical analysis of bone. What he has been able to do is to take Neandertal bone and study it for the so-called isotopic chemical signature of the foods that Neandertals have eaten.

This is a very promising, fairly new technology in biological anthropology, and what it suggests is that at least in Europe, and at least close to the 30,000-year-old time period, there is a lot of meat in Neandertal diet. So that, in combination with the tools that we see, the marks on the tools, the bones that are found and how they're processed, tells us that Neandertals were able to hunt successfully. It may well have been a type of close quarter, real confrontation type of hunting however, but they did it. They did it.

The most contentious area of interpretation about Neandertal behavior involves their cultural and symbolic behavior even more directly, and one of the most fascinating topics has to do with burial of the dead. This has not come up before because we've never had any hint at all that *Homo habilis*, *Homo erectus*, or any of the earlier hominids ever intentionally buried dead companions, but we do start to get that with Neandertals. Almost all biological anthropologists accept the fact that Neandertals, in at least some places, buried their dead. There is debate about, for example, a particular site here or a particular site there; how do you read this evidence in this case versus that case? But the fact of deliberate burial happening, at least in some places, is accepted.

A good example is the site of Shanidar in the country of Iraq. Shanidar is a cave site in a very mountainous area of Iraq, and what we find are multiple skeletons of Neandertal individuals in this cave, and at least four of them are quite clearly known to have been deliberate burials on the part of Neandertals. The more evidence that you can amass in any given case to suggest deliberate burial, the better, of course.

What archaeologists and biological anthropologists look for are things like dug graves, some very clear indentation in the soil that could have been made only by hominids, and also for a very careful positioning of the body in the grave. Oftentimes buried individuals were placed in a flexed position. This isn't always the case, but it is possible to tell when the body was strategically, and perhaps even tenderly—we don't know—placed in a grave.

Most useful are what we call *grave goods*, when some type of object was included along the individual upon burial. Examples here might be animal bones. There's one Neandertal burial where the person was buried with the jaw of a boar. There are sometimes stone slabs that are buried either with or on top of the individuals, and in Shanidar we have enough of the right mix of information to know that we're dealing with this type of burial.

Interestingly, when this site was first excavated by an American anthropologist in the 1970s, he could see that this was the case, that he was dealing with deliberate burials, but he also went a bit further, and he claims that there had been flowers put on the graves of the deceased individuals. He had found pollen in the cave and was able to say, he thought, that it was ancient pollen and that it reflected a variety of very colorful flower species, so when he reconstructed life of Neandertals in this cave, it got a little bit out of control. People were talking about the flower children and flower burials, and how emotional this must have been.

We know Shanidar had deliberate burials, that is not in question; but what has turned out to be the case, is that this pollen was not as ancient as first thought. The analysis and the dating of the pollen initially done in the '70s turned out to be inaccurate. It turns out that the pollen was much more recent, and in fact, was as likely to have been tracked in by rodents or even modern people as it was to have been old, so we have to let go of the flower burial part, but the rest of it stands up.

This leads to another issue, how do we really know what to make of the fact that Neandertals wanted to, and went about, and did bury individuals with whom they lived? What does it mean? Is this symbolic thinking, or what is it? I have recommended for you the video series that has been created by Don Johanson. You'll remember that he was the discoverer of Lucy in 1974. When, in his video series, he gets to the point of Neandertals, he is standing in a cave, and he talks about deliberate burial as a "powerfully spiritual act" on the part of Neandertals.

It's very intriguing, but I think perhaps a claim that we need to approach with caution. Consider the various levels of interpretation that we might make about Neandertal burial, or more precisely, about the meaning behind it. First of all, perhaps Neandertals realized through experience that it was simply more hygienic—healthier—to bury the dead rather than to leave the dead out in the open. Perhaps burial was an expression of respect or love or tender feelings or some type of emotional tie. That shouldn't surprise us given what we talked about, about even the apes having emotional ties.

Perhaps it did indicate some type of ritual or initial religion, but there is no way to know, and that's the point that I want to make here, that one explanation sounds as reasonable as another, and there's nothing in the bones or the graves or the grave goods that gives us an indicator of how we can interpret this Neandertal behavior. So I prefer to leave it as an open question, which I think is the best way to approach this.

What about art with Neandertals? Can we find symbolic thinking in representation of images or engraving or some type of art? Here, for one, the answer seems to be fairly clear, and the answer seems to be "no," that art appears in human evolutionary history only with *Homo sapiens*. There are just the slightest hints in some places of an engraving or a stone with lines on it, something like this, but there's nothing like the splendid, really artistic renderings that we will talk about coming into the picture with *Homo sapiens*.

So how do we sum up the major question about Neandertal symbolic or cultural behavior that we've been talking about in this section of the lecture? It doesn't seem as if the evidence for symbolic thinking is very strong. This does not mean that Neandertals lacked symbolic thinking. It's just hard to know from the evidence that we have.

Surely we can see behavior advances from, let's say, *Homo erectus*. The burial of the dead, particularly, is unprecedented in the fossil record at any other place; and the fact that there's such success at hunting, even in the absence of projectile weapons, is quite telling, as well. So we want to be able to talk about both things simultaneously, that there are new behaviors emerging with Neandertals without necessarily showing us that they are capable of a great deal of symbolism. That part will have to go unanswered, at least for now.

The precise relationship of the Neandertals to modern humans, and even to other hominids of this general time period, is another area that remains unclear. In these lectures, as we know, we will consider Neandertals as a separate species. We have explained that already. I should make a side note here and refer again to that textbook, the Jurmain et al. textbook that I have recommended as a companion for these lectures, because even there we see that those biological anthropologists came to the opposite conclusion. They are comfortable suggesting that Neandertals are part of our species, but just a variant type.

In that case, what biological anthropologists do is use different terminology. In that case, Neandertals become *Homo sapiens neandertalensis*—in other words, a sub-species—and we modern humans become *Homo sapiens sapiens*. This is the same type of taxonomic decision as was made for gorillas. There are gorillas that live in the lowlands of Africa and gorillas that live in the highlands, in the mountains. Most people are familiar with the highlands because of Dian Fossey's work. In any case, they are sub-species of the same species; and when biological anthropologists say "*Homo sapiens neandertalensis*," "*Homo sapiens sapiens*," what they're saying is exactly the same thing, that those two sets of creatures could have interbred with each other. That is something that I am not accepting and do reject.

Analysis of ancient DNA may someday resolve this question about same species or not the same species as modern humans. At present, I believe that the DNA analysis does support the fact that Neandertals should be considered a separate species; but there are, admittedly, uncertainties still surrounding this technique.

In the 1990s, a very exciting breakthrough was made, and DNA was extracted from Neandertal bones. Nicely enough, the skeleton that was used was the one discovered in 1856 in Germany, the very first

©2002 The Teaching Company.

Neandertal known to any of us. What happened was that the DNA was extracted and in the laboratory compared to DNA of modern humans, and this seemed to indicate, at least from what I can read of the technical literature, that in fact, Neandertals and modern humans could not interbreed and should be considered a separate species. There is argument over this point.

Let's broaden our view just a bit and look at this time period surrounding the Neandertals. What was going on between about 400,000 and 130,000 years ago? This is an area that we have kept somewhat fuzzy until now. We talked about *Homo erectus* as disappearing from the fossil record somewhere around 400-, 300-, 200,000, depending on how you define things.

There are, in fact, a group of hominids that are best just referred to as the *transitional hominids* that lived between about 400,000 and 130,000 years ago. They can be thought of as having a mix of *Homo sapiens* traits and *Homo erectus* traits, so when you hear the term "transitional hominid," you should translate that as *erectus/sapiens* mix. So there were a lot of different hominids in the world at this time, and they're considered in a group to be the *archaics*. In other words, just simply meaning that they're not modern humans.

Neandertals can be also called archaic, if you accept that they're *Homo neandertalensis*, as we are; but there are a lot of very shadowy relationships here that aren't entirely clear. Scientists are at work attempting to clarify the relationship of these species to each other— and particularly of Neandertals to *Homo sapiens*—and we will have to wait and see how that work goes. We'll talk a little bit more about it later, but there's not any big, startling conclusion that's coming here, because we simply don't know yet.

Neandertals, unsurprisingly I think, have been the most compelling of all of the hominids alive at this time period that approaches the appearance of modern humans, and I think that's because they are in some ways so close to us. We can so easily imagine a creature that hunted, dwelled in caves, and for whatever reason, buried their dead; but yet, when we look at them—or we look at depictions and representations of them more precisely—they loom very different from us. We know that they didn't have the symbolic capabilities that we did, so it's just a kind of mystery, shadowy sort of almost cousin type of creature.

Let's sum up this lecture, then. In the last century-and-a-half, Neandertal anatomy has come quite clearly into focus. We see these creatures as being robust in body, enormously strong, with big brains but fairly primitive faces, cold-adapted creatures. We are learning more about Neandertal behavior by the year. Some biological anthropologists feel comfortable assigning them fairly complex symbolic capabilities, others less so; but we can definitely see advances from *Homo erectus* in hunting, in their flake-efficient manufacture of tools, and in deliberate burial. What remains most unclear is this whole area of ancestral relationship among Neandertals, modern humans and other hominids, as well.

We want to return to the question of the origin of *Homo sapiens*, but we will not do so until Lecture Sixteen. The two intervening lectures are ones that I want to devote to behavioral issues that we have touched upon, but that I believe deserve further scrutiny. We will be talking about the role of hunting in human evolution and the reconstruction of gendered behavior in human evolution in Lectures Fourteen and Fifteen. So, we will start talking about hunting in the next lecture.

Lecture Fourteen
Did Hunting Make Us Human?

Scope:

In several previous lectures, we have noted that early *Homo* ate meat, obtaining it by processing animal carcasses with stone tools. But when did hominids turn from scavenging and opportunistic capture of small game to organized big-game hunting? Was hunting a "prime mover" of increased hominid brain size, as envisioned in classic early anthropological models?

In the late 1960s, two male anthropologists published a paper that was to remain influential for many years. This "Man the Hunter" paper claimed that hominid hunting, specifically the male-male cooperation seen as the heart of hunting, brought about great leaps in hominid problem solving and intelligence. The story of human evolution, in this view, was equated with the story of hunting.

Before long, some female anthropologists objected. What about the role of women in hominid food procurement, they asked? Female gathering of plant and vegetable material was likely far more crucial than hunting, they wrote, in bringing about increased intelligence and promoting the cohesion of social groups.

More recently, some anthropologists have challenged the hunting scenario from another quarter. They argue that hunting, as opposed to scavenging, developed too late in human evolution to have acted as a prime mover. A key question here is whether *Homo erectus* was primarily a scavenger or a hunter.

Although the "Man the Hunter" scenario in its starkest form has been rejected, echoes of the debate surrounding it may still be heard today. The biological anthropologist Craig Stanford has recently resurrected the role of meat-eating and meat-exchange as a prime mover in the story of human evolution. Taking a look at these various arguments, we will assess the degree to which hunting is a fundamental human adaptation.

Outline

I. We have seen that *Homo habilis* processed animal carcasses with Oldowan tools, and *Homo erectus* ate even more meat. We have remained agnostic, however, on the question of how this meat was procured, other than to suggest a role for scavenging. Several classic anthropological models have debated directly whether hunting was a prime mover in human evolution.

A. In the 1960s, Sherwood Washburn co-authored a seminal article with fellow anthropologist Chet Lancaster, claiming in no uncertain terms that hunting made humans human.

  1. Males are naturally drawn to hunting, these authors wrote. The skills of intelligence and cooperation required to bring off a successful hunt shaped the evolution of our species.

  2. In this scenario, females were painted as passive creatures who evolved on the "coattails" of the hunting males.

  3. Modern hunter-gatherer peoples were a referent for this type of model, but selectively so; the role of modern male hunters was emphasized.

B. Response to Washburn and Lancaster came from anthropologists writing in the 1970s, including Tanner and Zihlman, who believed that the female role in hominid evolution had been keenly undervalued.

  1. Tanner and Zihlman, among others, suggested that the gathering activity of females—collecting plants, tubers, and nuts—would have been more reliable and important than male hunting in hominid evolution.

  2. Using chimpanzees as referents, these female anthropologists argued that female hominids may have invented new tools to aid foraging in early human evolution. Thus, women would have been active, perhaps primary, contributors to the evolution of hominid intelligence and social cohesion.

  3. Ironically, Washburn and Lancaster's male-hunting model coincided with the publication of anthropological data showing that it is women's gathering activity that makes the major contribution to foraging in many hunter-gatherer peoples. These data supported Tanner and Zihlman.

II. In the next decades, the 1980s and 1990s, paleoanthropologists avidly sought hard evidence to shed light on the origins of human hunting. Early paleoanthropologists had been quick to equate any indicator of meat-eating with hunting. Paleoanthropologists were now more cautious.

A. Scavenging is an obvious alternative method for obtaining meat. Because hominid scavenging leaves marks on bones that look distinct from hunting marks, scientists can sometimes distinguish the two foraging strategies.

B. No hard evidence supports hunting in any australopithecine or in *Homo habilis*, though scavenging is indicated for *Homo habilis*.

C. Debate still surrounds the role of hunting versus scavenging in later hominids, such as *Homo erectus* and the transitional forms between *Homo erectus* and *Homo sapiens*. The clearest case for hunting can be made at the site of La Cotte de Saint-Brelade on the Channel Island of Jersey, which is associated with a transitional form appearing after *Homo erectus*.

D. The relatively late appearance of organized big-game hunting, coupled with the existence of cooperative small-game hunting in wild chimpanzees, leads many biological anthropologists to exclude hunting as a prime mover factor in human evolution.

III. Very recently, the biological anthropologist Craig Stanford has reinvigorated the debate about the significance of hunting in human evolution. He once again suggests that hunting has been of critical importance in early hominid evolution, but he does so in a new way.

A. For many years, Stanford studied chimpanzees at Gombe, Tanzania, becoming impressed by their skills in hunting red colobus monkeys.

B. Stanford suggests that chimpanzees make an excellent referential model for the origins of meat-eating and hunting in human evolution.

C. He stresses, however, not so much the act of hunting itself as the food-sharing that results when male hominids get meat. The strategic use by males of meat as currency when interacting with females is the key factor.

D. Response to Stanford's model varies. Whereas he insists that his model avoids the passive female stereotyping so pervasive in Washburn and Lancaster's, other anthropologists are not so sure.

IV. Looking back at the history of hunting models, we see shifts over time; the importance accorded to male hunting waxed and waned over the decades. Certainly, some of these shifts were brought about by new paleoanthropological and primatological evidence. However, less concrete factors also play a role, as we will examine in the next lecture.

Essential Reading:

De Waal, *Tree of Origin,* chapter by Stanford.

Questions to Consider:

1. In what ways does the recent Stanford scenario differ from Washburn and Lancaster's original formulation about hunting? Are any similarities evident between the two?

2. Why do you think hunting has been far more popular as a prime mover in evolutionary theories than has scavenging?

Lecture Fourteen—Transcript
Did Hunting Make Us Human?

We are now up to the point of origins of *Homo sapiens*, of modern humans. What we are going to do is take a step back for two lectures and talk about certain behavioral aspects of human evolutionary history, and we will start in this lecture with the evolution of hunting. We have already said that we know quite for certain that *Homo habilis* did process animal carcasses using Oldowan tools and then ate the meat. We know that *Homo erectus* ate even more meat than did *Homo habilis*.

Furthermore, we have credited the Neandertals with successful hunting behavior, but until the time period of the Neandertals—until our discussion of Neandertals—we have remained agnostic about the role of hunting in all of this meat acquisition; however, several classic anthropological models imputed hunting success to very early hominids, and went further and suggested that hunting was a real prime mover of human evolution. By a prime mover, it was meant that hunting actually accounted for brain size increases and increases in intelligence in the hominid lineage. We want to review some of these models and look at them with a more modern eye, with new evidence that has accumulated since they were first published.

In the 1960s, two authors collaborated on what has become a classic model of the evolution of hunting. The two authors were Sherwood Washburn and Chet Lancaster. We've already met Sherwood Washburn. Recall how influential he was when, in 1951, he made his call for the new physical anthropology. One of his students, also an anthropologist, is Chet Lancaster. They published this seminal article suggesting in no uncertain terms that it was hunting that made us human.

Their argument went like this. Males are naturally drawn to hunting. Hunting was a way of life from almost the start of the hominid time period. They went even further than to talk about the natural affinity of males for hunting. They talked also about the pleasurable basis of killing in warfare in general for males, whether in the past or in the present. They talked about a biological basis for pleasurable killing that is seen in the psychology of boys even today, in how easily they can be interested in things like hunting, in fishing, in sports, and in games of war.

They very specifically touch on one factor in hunting that made us human. This was the need for a lot of communication and cooperation during the hunt. So here's what we have: hunting as the human adaptation going back in hominid times, and it being a collective activity. We're talking here about big game hunting. We're not talking about walking through the bush and grabbing a rabbit. We're talking about hunting giraffe, elephant, and big game. This is not something that men—or anyone—could do individually, so it required, and put a premium, put a pressure on, communication and cooperation; and that's what did it for us, according to Washburn and Lancaster.

In this scenario published in 1968, females were painted as relatively passive creatures. Sure, they evolved—obviously, humans evolved as both males and females—but they evolved essentially on the coattails of the males. The males were doing all the work, and the females kind of coasted along, if you will. More to the point, they were pretty invisible. It's easy enough to look at this askance now. I am quite sympathetic to feminist anthropology. I read a lot of the feminist literature, and I know that this doesn't sound right. This absence of females doesn't sound right.

But we have to be careful here, and not too easily mock a past scenario, because at the time, some of this made more sense than it sounds like it should today. Modern hunter-gatherers were the referent for this model. Washburn and Lancaster looked at the date from modern forager peoples who were living off the land before agriculture and before domestication. We've encountered this type of model before.

This is the same type of thing that Glyn Isaac did when he wanted to model *Homo habilis* food sharing and *Homo habilis* base camp living, so Washburn and Lancaster went to the anthropological source data, but they did so selectively. There was information—as we'll hear in a minute—about females, but there was more information about male hunting and the importance of this. This is what they chose to focus on.

This scenario, as it was published, made a very big splash in the anthropological world. In fact, it is still reprinted today in classic collections of important anthropological models. Partly, I believe, this is because Washburn was, after all, a major figure in the field, but this is not to say that there was no response.

There was a backlash to this model, starting probably in the 1970s, and two of the prominent counter-modelers, if you will, were Tanner and Zihlman. Nancy Tanner was the first anthropologist who was instrumental in leading the charge against the male hunting model. She unfortunately died fairly early in her life and in her career. Her co-author was Adrienne Zihlman, who is still an influential biological anthropologist today. She's at the University of California, Santa Cruz.

Together, what they wanted to do was reinsert women back into this role of the evolution of hominids and the evolution of human intelligence. What they suggested is that, in fact, the gathering activity of females would be the most important factor, rather than male hunting. Gathering is walking long distances if necessary to collect plant material, highly caloric and nutritious nuts, possibly even eggs of birds and small mammals if they're very small, but whatever can be done while walking and gathering food, putting it in some kind of a basket or a sling, and coming back to wherever the people are about to eat. Tanner and Zihlman said that it was critical to see the role of women, not only to balance out what males were doing, but also to see the role of women as primary in understanding human evolution.

They had two sources for their own support for their own model. The first support that they used was data from chimpanzees. We know that in chimpanzees there's a differential pathway, by sex, to acquisition of protein. Male chimpanzees do the vast majority of hunting, and the female chimpanzees really concentrate on acquiring protein through tool use. They sit for possibly hours at a time getting termites out of mounds and cracking open hard-shelled nuts. This type of work is much more compatible with raising infants, with having young, dependent infants with them. So Tanner and Zihlman said we need to look back at chimpanzees as a referent, possibly for the common ancestor, to see that females were using tools very heavily and might have been inventing those tools.

Their second source of data was at the other end of the continuum, if you will, and they, too, wanted to look at contemporary foraging people just as Washburn and Lancaster had, but here they said a careful look at the data suggests that women are the ones really holding things together. In fact, the literature did reflect this at the time, so it's not entirely clear why Washburn and Lancaster didn't take this into account.

Among certain forager groups for example, yes, there's a lot of hunting, but hunting is quite risky. You go out and you look for game, but the game is moving and defending itself. You may or may not succeed in bringing down big game and getting that big payoff. So hunting was conceived of as both a high-risk strategy and high payoff when it succeeds.

By contrast, gathering is not so risky. After all, the plants are not moving around, nor are the nuts, and they don't attempt to defend themselves. One might have to walk a long way to find the appropriate resources, but there they are; so every few days you could go and simply get a good source of nutrition.

It was somewhat ironic, because Washburn and Lancaster's model appeared really at about the same time as the initial push in the anthropological literature suggesting the importance of the female gathering role, and that data really supported Tanner and Zihlman, so there was essentially a polite, and in some cases not so polite, fight breaking out in the literature. Others also joined in to say, "Wait a minute. This focus on hunting may not be as accurate as it first seemed to some."

The decades went on, and in the 1980s and the 1990s, paleoanthropologists wanted to get some hard evidence to really look at hunting and what role hunting might have played in human evolution. For example, it is possible to look at tools, as we have already hinted, and to ask what clues they reveal to us about hunting, and to keep in mind an alternative hypothesis that meat might have been acquired by scavenging, something that we have talked about. Hominid scavenging simply means going up and disarticulating a carcass of an animal that's already dead—possibly killed by big cats or other predators, possibly animals that dropped dead of natural causes.

Sometimes the tool marks on the bone can allow paleoanthropologists to distinguish scavenging from hunting. If you think about it, if you come across a bone, and there are overlaid on top of carnivore teeth marks hominid tool marks, this is a good clue that the animal in question was killed by the carnivore, the big cat, say a leopard, and then secondarily, the hominids would have scavenged from that situation. If the reverse should be true, and there are hominid tool marks right down at the level of the bone, either with carnivore marks overlaying them or with no marks at all overlaying them, hunting would be more likely.

Using this method, which again works on some bones but not all, we can say that there's no hard evidence of hunting, from this or really any other source of information, for australopithecines or for *Homo habilis*. It's a little bit more questionable in *Homo erectus*, but still nothing particularly clear with the *Homo erectus* time point. We already know that Neandertals did hunt; but in fact, if we look at this transitional time period, what we've been admitting is a kind of fuzzy time period of the transitional hominids.

We can find a site that is typically considered to be the earliest clear-cut evidence for real, good hunting in hominids. This site is dated to approximately 250,000 years ago; again associated with the transitional hominid. The name of the site is La Cotte de Saint-Brelade. It's on the Channel Island of Jersey, which is off the coast of France. What you find here are mammoth bones and rhino bones at the bottom of a cliff, mixed in with hominid tools, with clear marks from the tools on the bones.

Another thing that's very important to mention is that the animals that are in this assemblage, the rhino and the mammoth, are in many cases *prime age*, and here is something that separates this bone assemblage out from what we've been talking about before. By prime age, I mean that adults in the prime of life were killed. It is not just that older animals, which might be tired and sick, or the very young, vulnerable animals were killed—which might indicate more of a scavenging idea, because those are the types of animals that big cats can kill—rather, the really strong animals were killed.

Clearly, you've got a big cliff and a bunch of animals at the bottom of it. This indicates that there was likely a driving sort of hunting strategy, by which I mean driving the animals off the cliff, and then butchering them at the bottom. That's hunting. That is fully counting as hunting.

So we have then, transitional hominid hunting. Later on, we have Neandertal hunting. If you take this data, this data that suggests a relatively late appearance of organized big game hunting, you can put them together with the data from chimpanzees. We know, after all, that chimpanzees hunt not big game but small game in organized ways without tools. Both of these things together have tended to push biological anthropologists away from thinking of hunting as a real push factor in human evolution; and remember, what we're trying to explain is fairly early hominid brain size increase—as with early *Homo*—and early pushes for intelligence.

But, as with most things in this field, the debate is not over. In fact, there's a biological anthropologist who has quite recently reinvigorated the debate about the evolution of human hunting, and this is Craig Stanford. He suggests, once again, that hunting *was* an important prime mover early on, but he does so with an interesting twist that pushes us to examine his idea quite closely.

Craig Stanford, I should add, knows very well that when he resurrects the evolution of hunting as a prime mover, he is going to be put automatically in the camp with Washburn and Lancaster, or people will try to do that. So when he writes, he explicitly says in his writing, here's how Washburn and Lancaster were right, and here's how they were wrong. He bases his scenario upon some of their work, but is quite careful to distance himself in other ways.

Let's start at the beginning. For many years, Stanford was doing primatology research at the site of Gombe, Tanzania, which, as we know, was where Jane Goodall has conducted her decades-long study of chimpanzees. Stanford's specialty was to study the hunting behavior of these chimpanzees. He was quite impressed with the efficiency of this hunting, which we have already talked about in earlier lectures. You might remember that the males are the ones who do hunt; that specifically, adult and adolescent males working together conduct 90 percent of the hunts at Gombe.

Stanford suggests—against the popular tide now—that chimpanzees do make a good referential model for understanding the role of human hunting in evolution. So he is going against the grain in two ways, in that he wants to look at hunting, and that he wants to do so with a referential model; and you'll recall from earlier on, I had said that a lot of people are moving away from that one-to-one type of comparison. But he does a very good job of suggesting that a referential model works in this case because of how sophisticated chimpanzees are in their hunting.

Stanford also says that it is a false dichotomy to set up a kind of scavenging versus hunting situation. He sees no reason to do this. The question that he would prefer we ask would be, to what degree did early hominids scavenge, and to what degree did they hunt? He says that it doesn't have to be one or the other. I find it intriguing that he says this because chimpanzees actually just hunt and don't scavenge at all. We have never known any chimpanzees to scavenge, but beyond that, his point probably stands.

What Stanford stresses though, is not the same thing that Washburn and Lancaster stressed. He's not so interested in the cooperation and communication that takes place during the hunt—when there's actual pursuit of prey—rather, he's interested in what happens after, when the meat is acquired and it's about to be shared. To be specific, the strategic use of meat as currency when males interact with females is his single-most key factor.

What Stanford says is that meat is a kind of political tool, and that figuring out what to do with the meat when you've got it is what leads us to be able to appreciate hunting as a prime mover. So meat is now currency, and what males do with it is based on what he has seen chimpanzee males do with their meat. Primarily, two important things can happen with the meat. First, the meat can be shared with estrous females. In chimpanzees now, we're talking about females with sexual swellings, those females that are visibly marked as being ready to be impregnated and capable of conception.

In chimpanzees again, males will also distribute meat to political supporters, the chimps that have helped them rise in the hierarchy, or they might want to help them in the future. So there's a consolidation of power in the male hierarchy going on, and there is basically trading of meat for sexual favors.

Stanford says we can apply this to hominids. We don't know that there were hominid females with sexual swellings, but adapting to the physiology of hominids, what we would get then are males who are thinking strategically about how to use their food, their meat that they've gotten, to make gains for themselves.

The response to Stanford's model has varied. It hasn't been out all that many years. The book on which it was based came out in the very late 1990s, so it's still taking some time to be fully responded to by other anthropologists, but there is one issue that's been tending to get a fair amount of attention. Stanford insists that he has avoided, with his model, passive female stereotyping. In other words, we know that Washburn and Lancaster were rather roundly assailed for leaving women out, for focusing only on the males, and for essentially constructing a coattails theory where females only evolved because males evolved.

Some anthropologists said, "Doesn't this seem like what Stanford is doing, too?" Stanford very quickly says no, because he knows that he cannot be tarred with that brush. That would be very bad. He says, in fact, that there is a role for being tactical and strategic for females in his model, because after all, the females want to get meat, so they want to maneuver themselves with the individual males who have the meat to give. So it is a reciprocal process, he stresses. I could point out in his book that he stresses this in right about three pages out of several hundred pages, so there is this question: Is he saying this part about the females because he really had better, or does he truly balance the roles of males and females? This is an open question.

He does mention, by the way, a very intriguing fact about chimpanzees. He's always working back and forth between chimps and the purported behavioral aspects of hominids. He says that another researcher at Gombe found that female reproductive success of chimps goes up when they do acquire a lot of meat from males; and that immediately should ring bells for you, reproductive success is important to this course. So, if there is a real benefit to females to getting this meat that also translates to reproductive success in hominid females, then maybe there really was maneuvering on the part of females, and then it is possible to come out with a balanced model.

But as I said, anthropologists aren't so sure if that's really what Stanford intended or not. So it is important to note that there's a difference in the factor that we're focusing on. We don't want to leap from Washburn and Lancaster to Stanford and say that it's all continuous and all talking about human hunting. This would be unfair to Stanford because of the fact that he's really talking about intelligence, cognition and strategizing in a very, very different way than the earlier model ever did.

Still, if we take a look back over the decades since 1968, what we can see is some continuity and some shift over time in the importance that has been accorded to hunting. It has tended to wax and wane over the various decades. One thing that I have wondered a lot about is the fact that we have Washburn and Lancaster really touting the role of hunting; we have Stanford bringing back the role of hunting; and we have Tanner and Zihlman talking about female gathering. What strikes you about this dichotomy—if we can make two basic groups of theories—is that Washburn, Lancaster and Stanford are male, and Tanner and Zihlman are female. The males are emphasizing the male role in human evolution. The females are emphasizing the female role in human evolution.

Adrienne Zihlman, in fact—I've mentioned that she's still an active and important anthropologist—has made quite a name for herself in pushing back, if you will, against male-centered models of human evolution. She has even asked, "How come we're all so sure that Lucy, the three-million-year-old hominid dubbed Lucy by Don Johanson, is really a female?" "If you think about it," she says, "Lucy was the very first creature of *Australopithecus afarensis* ever to be discovered. By definition, this is a discovery point, so how did Johanson know there's no array of skeletons for comparison? How did he look at this single initial pelvis for a new species and decide that she's female?"

Zihlman, at one point, became quite notorious because she was hosting a conference in which she wanted to talk about some of these exciting issues in human evolution, and she issued invitations only to women, and she barred men from attending, so we might ask whether that's a fair strategy or not. She said she wanted "reasoned discourse," and she would invite only women, so I'll leave it to you to decide if that is fair. But we want to wonder, perhaps, about the role of the actual authors of these models, the role of their gender and whether that plays in here.

Certainly, I don't want to go too far with this. It is absolutely true that paleoanthropological and primatological advances have brought some of this waxing and waning that I've talked about about. We couldn't have gotten Stanford's model without years of careful study of chimpanzee hunting. We couldn't be talking, as we are now, about the possible alternative of scavenging unless we had the new technology that allowed us to really analyze hominid tools and the so-called "cut marks" on those tools to which was primary: the carnivore teeth marks or the hominid tool marks.

So all of that is very important, and I would add as an aside here that this is a particularly good lecture to bring back in a statement I made earlier that relates to the importance of primate studies to biological anthropology because, think what Stanford did here. He was lucky enough to go to Gombe as a student and study chimpanzees, but he didn't just study them for chimp hunting and stop there.

He wanted to take that data and apply it to something that would illuminate human prehistory, so he published his data on chimpanzee hunting. He involved other primatologists who worked at other chimp sites or possibly at baboon sites— we remember that baboons have, in the past, hunted—to get a conversation going about hunting at the primate level. Then he began to use a referential model to extend that conversation to paleoanthropologists, and to talk about whether or not chimps can really tell us something about how humans might have hunted, and then also the sociocultural anthropologists were brought in, because we know that the data on modern human foragers is so important.

So I find it particularly satisfying that Washburn is at one and the same time the author of this initial model that kicked off all of this discussion about the role of hunting, and also was the one who really wanted primate studies to play this role in anthropology, for the comparative research to turn out to really mean something and to lead us to conclusions about human behavior. So it is quite fascinating to consider a host of reasons for what turns out to be a kind of pendulum swing about the role of hunting: first, the certain statement that it was important, then the backlash, and now a reconsideration in a different format.

The issue of gender is so important that I think it deserves a lecture of its own, not so much the importance of the authors' gender in making models, but on a wider sort of perspective: the question of whether there might be societal factors that help shape how gender gets incorporated into models of human evolution. We're going to talk about this when we come back and we start Lecture Fifteen. We will revisit different models of human evolutionary history and we will see how gender fits in as a factor.

Lecture Fifteen
The Prehistory of Gender

Scope:

Biological anthropologists have hotly contested the relative roles of men and women in human prehistory, as the previous lecture on hunting versus gathering attests. From our current vantage point, it becomes clear that some important models of the evolution of human behavior were constrained by assumptions particular to American culture in the 1960s and 1970s. The nuclear family was, for instance, assumed to be the typical family structure in hominid evolution by some anthropologists; the male "producer" (food provider) was depicted as giving food and other aid to the female "reproducer" (breeder).

Such a simplistic scenario, we now see, does not fit with the cross-cultural data on human families. Neither does this scenario square with the evidence from primate studies showing that female monkeys and apes are capable of producing food for themselves and caring for their offspring without assistance from males. And if hominid females needed aid because their reproductive profiles differ from those of monkeys and apes, were males really the sole available source for that aid?

As assailable as male-dominated models, however, are scenarios of human evolution that depict females in control. No evolutionary validity is gained by transforming male-centered into female-centered models. The most credible schemes are those that emphasize flexibility in gender roles according to local resources and local environmental circumstances.

Outline

I. Paleoanthropological models by necessity involve interpretation (see Lecture Eight); the relatively sparse bones and artifacts of human evolution must be fleshed out. In turn, scientists' interpretations are shaped by the time and place in which they think and write. This may be especially true when it comes to interpretations of gender.

    A. Anatomical differences based on sex, that is, sexual dimorphism in male and female skeletons, may fossilize. It is often possible to distinguish skeletons by sex and to make inferences about different levels of strength, or variation in diet, between males and females.

B. Behavioral differences based on sex do not fossilize. Few other clues exist as to which sex hunted, or cooked, or made tools—or whether both sexes may have carried out these activities. In the absence of hard evidence, paleoanthropologists turn to ethnographic evidence from living modern peoples.

C. In selecting the data to use, and in combining different sources of data, subjectivity inevitably plays a role. An individual scientist's preconceptions about gender may creep into his or her model, perhaps unconsciously. As a quick example, we will analyze the museum diorama depicting two bipedal australopithecines leaving footprints in African ash more than 3.5 million years ago.

II. We will analyze in-depth three prominent paleoanthropological models, one already encountered and two new ones, that touch on gender roles. Our focus in each will involve the roles accorded to the hominid male and the nuclear family.

A. As we have seen, Washburn and Lancaster's hunting model from 1968 gives to the hominid male the primary evolutionary role, deemphasizing the female's role. Significantly, it also projects the nuclear family millions of years back into the past.

B. Thirteen years later, in 1981, Owen Lovejoy published a much-touted scenario in which the role of hunting was minimized. Males were still the evolutionary prime movers, though; mobile males were naturally selected to provision sedentary females and offspring. The nuclear family is as prominently placed in this model as in Washburn and Lancaster's.

C. In 2001, Richard Wrangham and colleagues suggested that cooking food over a controlled fire outweighs hunting as a prime mover in human evolution. Females are active in this model because they are the ones who cook. Males, however, must protect females from potential theft of cooked resources by other "scrounger" males. Once again, the nuclear family reappears.

D. All three models imply that hominid females would have pair-bonded with males because they require male protection to ensure their survival and reproductive success. How valid is this perspective?

1. Primate studies tell us that female primates are capable of both reproduction (of offspring) and production (of food for themselves); males do not provision females in monkeys and apes.

2. As life spans lengthened, however, hominid females would have become responsible for feeding their juveniles, as well as their infants. Hominid females may well have needed aid, then, to cope with an increased reproductive burden. Yet equating aid with male protection may be unnecessarily constraining.

3. Anthropologists have long known that the nuclear family is a minority pattern across the globe; it is now the minority pattern even in American society.

4. Gender patterns in American society may have influenced the models' authors in their willingness to draw conclusions about males and females in our distant past.

III. When anthropologists turn the tables on these male-dominant models and prioritize hominid females instead, rejecting the nuclear family in the process, no scientific validity is gained.

A. The models put forth by Tanner and Zihlman simply reverse the prevailing assumptions about gender. Females become more important evolutionarily than males, and female-centered networks are favored over the nuclear family.

B. Little support exists for models that privilege strict "behavioral sorting" by gender. Ethnographic data show that a variety of roles may be played by men and women and that a variety of social units may provide a society's base.

C. The best solution may be to offer alternative behavioral scenarios that all recognize the inherent variation within genders. Referential, phylogenetic, or conceptual models from primates; paleoanthropological evidence from skeletons and behavioral artifacts; and ethnographic analogies may all be used.

Essential Reading:

De Waal, *Tree of Origin,* chapter by Wrangham.

Supplementary Reading:

Jolly, *Lucy's Legacy.*

Questions to Consider:

1. What data support a shift in focus on hunting as prime mover to cooking as prime mover in human evolution?

2. What part can studies of monkeys and apes play in fashioning solid models of hominid gender roles?

Lecture Fifteen—Transcript
The Prehistory of Gender

In Lecture Fifteen, we will confront a layer of interpretation that is underneath the layer that we talked about before with hunting models, and I'm referring here to gender; or to put it informally, in human evolution, which sex is doing what, anyway? We really would like to know what males and females were doing in the human evolutionary past. By now in this course, it is old hat to refer to the fact that paleoanthropological interpretations are necessary to understand human evolution. We have some bones and we have some artifacts, but what we really need to do is to flesh out those bones, if you will. Excuse the pun.

In turn, the scientists that are doing the interpretation are shaped by the time, place and culture in which they live. We tend to think of science as objective. If you ask children, for example, what is their view of the scientist, they always draw for you a picture of somebody in a white coat looking very serious and describe the idea that scientists are out to get at the truth, and they can uncover the truth. Of course, there's truth to that statement, as well. We know that the scientific method exists because science values objectivity, testability, and the whole process of evidence gathering that we have talked about.

But the types of things that we are interested in in this part of the course absolutely require modeling, and we've been through this before, so we know that is the fact. What we want to talk about is what other factors, societally, might impinge upon models, and I would make the claim that it is at least a defensible hypothesis that models about gender might fall into this arena more so than others. In other words, they might more so be prone to being affected by societal trends and preconceptions about gender.

Let's start at the easiest starting place, and that would be looking for anatomical differences divided by sex in the human fossil record. Here you have something concrete and material. What you want to do is look at male skeletons, compare them to female skeletons, and chart the differences between them to see if they might have any significance behaviorally. So what we're asking about is sexual dimorphism, asking about whether they were two forms anatomically, one for each sex, and we know already that there were sexual dimorphic hominids.

In the time period of australopithecines and *Homo habilis*, the consensus is that males were quite a bit bigger and heavier than females, more so than we see today with modern *Homo sapiens*. There seems to have been a shift point at the very same place that we've been calling a shift point all along, *Homo erectus*, with a reduction in sexual dimorphism at that period. That is an interesting fact to start with.

We can also look at skeletons, sort them by male versus female using the pelvis usually, and ask about whether there's a difference in strength indicated in one versus the other, and possibly differences in diet. We had talked earlier about the robust australopithecines as being specialized hominids, having this crushing and grinding complex of the jaws and the skull that allowed them to eat hard foods, nuts and fruit that were very, very hard to open, as opposed to the gracile hominids. It seems clear that the crushing and grinding complex was more exacerbated in the male hominids than in the female hominids, and we know that again, by this process of anatomical sorting by sex. So this goes on all the time.

It's when we get to questions of behavioral sorting that we run into problems, because the sort of information that we need simply does not fossilize. We have few clues as to, for example, which sex would have made tools: Oldowan tools, hand axes, flake tools. How do we know which sex might have hunted? This is still an open question. We know from modern ethnographic data that there are some—few, but some—populations in which females do play an active role in hunting; for example, in the Philippines.

Artwork—any number of things—we could ask about and we don't have a way to trace back a difference by sex; so in the absence of this evidence, we turn to modeling, as you know. If we think creatively, we'd like to be able to fall back on evidence. For example, we'd like to say maybe grave goods of Neandertals could give us a clue; but if you really analyze what these data tell us, it is still hard to get concretely at gender.

Let's say you look at a deliberate burial, what we have quite recently talked about in this course at Shanidar Cave, and you find that a Neandertal was deliberately buried with a tool. Does that necessarily mean that that individual made the tool? I would submit that there are alternative ideas; for example, that the tool might have been a gift to the individual, it might have been buried with that skeleton as a sign of respect or affection.

So again, we can't even look later on in the time period of human evolution for easy clues to gender, much less at the beginning time periods. In selecting the data to use, and in combining different sources of data, we do know that subjectivity plays a role. Again, I want to be very clear that I'm not suggesting that scientists would ever consciously manipulate data; but rather we're talking at the level of preconception or of assumption, and the basic, guiding theme of this lecture will be that gender falls prey to this.

To start off with a quick example before we get into more detailed ones. I'd like to describe for you a diorama that can be seen at the American Museum of Natural History in New York. This is a wonderful museum, as anyone who has been there can attest. There have been very spectacular exhibits related to human evolution. At one point, an exhibit was mounted called "Ancestors," in which all the original dug-up skeletons of hominids were brought in one place—from East Africa, from Europe, from Asia—not casts, not replicas, but almost all of the original bones. Being in that room was really quite a moving thing, a moving event, and an experience for many of us.

But there is also there, as a permanent fixture, a diorama; and what it shows us are two hominids, a male and a female, in a particular pose. In order to describe this, I need to give you some background. The hominids in question are *Australopithecus afarensis*—in other words, those hominids of which Lucy is a part—and they're depicting bipedal walking across the African savannah with a volcano in the background.

We know that in 1977, there was a very great discovery that backed up what we had already learned by that point about *afarensis* bipedalism. This was at the site of Mary Leakey in Laetoli, Tanzania, East Africa, and what were found were trails of footprints, of hominids, of birds, of elephants, of creatures great and small, in other words.

What had happened was that there was a volcanic explosion with ash laid down, and then all these creatures walked across this area, and then after their footprints were laid down, a second volcano exploded, sealing the footprints, making them, first of all, clearly and easily datable, and second, clearly and easily analyzable. The date for the footprints is 3.6 million years ago, found in association also with *afarensis* bones, so we know what we're talking about.

We are, of course, going to focus on the hominid footprints, not the birds and the elephants. What we see in the structure of the foot in this footprint trail is a clearly bipedal foot with the toes all in line, one with the other, and a clear heel of a biped—no question about that.

However, what was a little bit more ambiguous was the fact that there were two trails of hominid footprints next to each other, one trail with a slightly bigger foot, one with a slightly smaller, and it was the job of the museum to depict what might have happened as hominids strolled across the savannah 3.6 million years ago. What the diorama shows is that the reconstructor decided to put a male and a female walking side by side, a couple, a pair-bond, apparently. The male had his arm around the female's shoulders in the diorama—and presumably in prehistory—and also, the female had her head turned, her face turned, and her mouth opened a little bit, gazing a little bit out into the distance.

Think about this: a male and a female, with the male protectively draping an arm around the female; not, for example, two women walking across the savannah, one slightly taller; not two men walking, one slightly taller; not a man or a woman and a juvenile or a teenager or an adolescent; but a male and a female with this protective embrace. By the way, you can judge for yourself if you can go to see it, but the expression on the female's face cannot easily be interpreted as an entirely clever one. She looks just a little bit vacant-eyed.

There is, I would think, some kind of preconception here. Out of all the possible scenarios to choose, what was chosen? A pair-bonded male and female. I suppose you could argue that they could be brother and sister, as well; but there certainly is something to be said for the pair-bond idea, and the question that this raises, I hope, is obvious: why pick that for the diorama, versus all the others?

Let's go into some more detail now, and let's analyze three prominent paleoanthropological models that turn on this question of gender. One model we have already encountered; two new ones that I will discuss, we have not yet talked about. Our focus in each one is going to be on the role of the male and the role of the so-called *nuclear family.* So we're not going to be talking a lot about hunting, but rather, gender roles; and specifically, the evolution of the family. To start with, I should clarify what I mean by the nuclear family, and I'm talking here about the so-called typical American family: two parents and children living in one household together—not an extended family, in other words.

The first model we'll discuss is the one we have already talked about, the Washburn and Lancaster, 1968. Primarily, yes, this model was about hunting—for males, the primary significance for driving human evolution—but it also and significantly projected far back into the past the nuclear family. In fact, Washburn and Lancaster say that hunting and the providing of meat to females by males created the human family, and they mean, they clearly say, "nuclear family" here. So there is an extra bit to the scenario that we didn't get to talk about: that because the male is able to take this role, because he is then able to provide, the family forms around this activity, and this is another aspect to the model.

Thirteen years later, 1981 rolls around, and another important model gets published, this by the anthropologist/anatomist Owen Lovejoy. It was published in the journal *Science.* Owen Lovejoy I have mentioned before, but not by name. When I was talking about Don Johanson bringing back his very first discovery made in Ethiopia, that bipedal knee, back to the United States and laying it out on the carpet of an American anatomist at home to ask, "Is it really bipedal?"—that was Owen Lovejoy.

He published a suggestion that, in fact, we need to stop focusing so much on hunting. In other words, he was part of the backlash to Washburn and Lancaster. He talked instead about what's called the *male provisioning model.* He said that, yes, males did need to provide females with resources, but that it wasn't through hunting. It was through other means, through ranging widely over the landscape and bringing food back to a relatively stationary female and dependent offspring.

By the way, this really is a model that's about the evolution of bipedalism. The fact that the male is provisioning the female was interpreted as a selection pressure on male mobility that would increase the efficiency of bipedalism, so we can count this as one of a number of push factors that have been modeled for bipedalism; but for our particular purposes, what we want to focus on is the idea that a family resulted, the nuclear family. Because the male is in charge and is actively provisioning the family, the family was able to spring up, and in this particular way, there is continuity from Washburn and Lancaster, although there's not continuity in other ways.

Let's jump ahead to the year 2001 and the third model. Here, Richard Wrangham and his colleagues published a model that has gotten huge attention. The *Science Times*, that section every Tuesday of the *New York Times*, has featured it. Many science sites on the web and science magazines have discussed this, and it has been published more formally, as well. They suggested that the prime mover factor in human evolution is not hunting, but is cooking.

Controlled fire would lead to the ability to cook foods, and they tie this development to the time period of *Homo erectus*. They believe that *Homo erectus* had the ability to control fire, an issue we touched on earlier. They say that cooking would have really opened up the diet for hominids, and would have made tough foods easier to process and digest, would have allowed high quality foods to be put into the diet in new ways, and calories and nutrition released into the hominid diet in new ways.

They suggest that this also might explain why, in fact, the levels of sexual dimorphism do reduce at the time period of *Homo erectus*. It appears that female body size gets bigger at this time to close that gap in height and weight between male and female hominids, and what they suggest is that this extra quality in nutrition particularly impacted hominid females and allowed them to get bigger.

In the Wrangham et al. model, we see that hominid females are pretty active. In fact, they're the ones who get to do the cooking. You can decide whether this is a good thing to do, to assign the cooking to hominid females; and by that I mean, do we have enough evidence to suggest that that's really true?

But again, for our purposes, we want to focus on a particular segment of the model, and that is the part of the model called the *theft hypothesis*. What these researchers say is that this cooking, this new development in human evolution, would have forced females to bond with males, specifically to get protection from scrounging; that there would be some labor exploiters—essentially, some individuals, whether male or female—who would have attempted to steal cooked food rather than getting it and cooking it on their own. They would be attempting to steal this from the females; and as a result then, the females need the protection of males. Here, once again, the nuclear family begins to appear.

Of course, Wrangham and his colleagues have not pushed the nuclear family back quite so far in time as the other two models that we've discussed have, but it is still there in a central part. So there is some robust continuity across the three models. They all imply that hominid females were forced to pair bond with males because they required something from males: protection or resources for the females' own survival and reproductive success.

How valid is this perspective? Again, as we have said in relation to other debates, certainly this is a possible scenario. Any of them are possible. But is it likely? Let's bring to bear some sources of information to assess this continuity in the models about the need for males. We can look at three sources of information that may help us.

First, primate studies. We learn from primatology, when we look at monkeys and apes, that females are quite capable of simultaneous production and reproduction. What I mean by this is that females forage for themselves, nurse their infants, and reproduce, all without aid from males. There are some cases in which paternal care does exist. They're rare for monkeys and apes. There are some cases in which males take care of infants and may even feed infants, but there is no suggestion that there is male provisioning of females at any point from primatology.

However, the second source of data tells us that we had better not stop just by looking at monkeys and apes. We know from paleoanthropological study that life spans lengthened during hominid evolution. We know that life stages got longer, too. At some point, infancy became longer than what we see in great apes, and a juvenile stage became important.

The anthropologists Lancaster and Lancaster—names you've heard before, Jane Lancaster and Chet Lancaster—have been quite influential in pointing out that hominid females at some point would have had multiple dependent offspring, not what we see in apes when you have one infant, take care of it for a long time, suckle it for a long time, and wean it when you're about to have another, but rather, having a juvenile to feed while you're nursing a small infant.

In other words, there may have been a shift during human evolution that required some kind of resource provisioning of the female, over and above the situation that you would see with an ape female.

The question now becomes, is there any necessary need that this would have resulted in a male-female pair bond or a nuclear family? Maybe yes, maybe no. We will find out in a minute that there are alternative scenarios. We can certainly think of kin groups of females, for example, helping out a female who might need aid in order to continue her life and have reproductive success. So the suggestion made here is that the need for male protection, specifically, might be unnecessarily constraining in the models that we have talked about.

The third source of data we can bring to bear is from sociocultural anthropology and from demographic data that is more recent. Anthropologists have known for a long time that the nuclear family is not the dominant family pattern around the globe. We know that extended families are quite common. In some cases, there may be multiple wives—in other words, a polygamist family situation. In other cases, it may be the grandparental generation living with the family so that there's a big extended family. So nuclear families do not seem to be what is found across the world.

We also have learned much more recently that the nuclear family, however mythical in our understanding of America, is actually the minority pattern in American society now. If you look at data from the 2000 census in the United States—it is now being thoroughly analyzed, and it's fascinating to look at this relatively new data— what we can learn is that 24 percent of American households are now the "typical" configuration, the nuclear family, and the typical is in quotes because we assume that it's typical; but in fact, it's less than a quarter of American households. That is down fairly appreciably from the percentage in 1970. Forty percent of American households in 1970 were nuclear family households. By the way, right now—or in 2000, more specifically—25 percent of American households are single-person households, a single person.

It is always tricky to work with statistics, and I should be careful to clarify. It is also true—we know this from the same census data— that now in the United States, fully 70 percent of dependent children alive today live with two parents, so there's another way to look at this. But at the very same time, those two-parent households are likely to be composed of two parents who work, and a lot of stepparents are involved, so it is not the biological nuclear family in quite a few cases, of two biological parents with two biological children.

In any case, what we begin to see is that the nuclear family was pushed back in time with reasons that don't always dovetail with just science. In other words, the question that I think is worth raising is whether gender patterns within American society might have influenced models such as Washburn and Lancaster, or Lovejoy, or even Wrangham more recently.

Certainly, when Washburn and Lancaster wrote, it was 1968. You can't find a better emblematic year for a time of social change and social upheaval in this country. This was a time when the women's movement was underway as well as other sorts of social protest. There was still, to some degree, an expectation of the woman as nurturer and the man as provider—not wholly, not in every segment of society, certainly. I don't want to go too far with this, but it is worth thinking that this may be a partial explanation.

Another reason why we shouldn't go too far with this is there were other alternatives offered to the nuclear family. Not everybody was suggesting the antiquity of the nuclear family or the importance of the male providing. We can return here to Tanner and Zihlman for this type of model. Here, we already know that these anthropologists have turned the tables around from a significance of male resource acquisition to significance of female resource acquisition; and I would suggest that, when the tables are simply flipped and females are made primary, that no scientific validity is gained.

In other words, it's not simply that Tanner and Zihlman wish to redress an imbalance. They don't simply say, "Look, these models have been missing the boat because they leave females out." What they do is they empower females to the extent of making males nearly invisible. Tanner and Zihlman talk about females as inventors of tools; females as the stable, reliable food providers; networks of females and female relatives surrounding a reproductive female, perhaps in place of the nuclear family. What you get here is a substitution of what you had before. You had before, the primacy of the male. Now you have the primacy of the female. Clearly, in neither of these situations is there balance.

Little support exists for this type of behavioral sorting by gender. We know that ethnographic data should teach us this lesson if we look again, cross-culturally, as anthropologists are so good at doing. We know that a variety of roles—just looking at foraging—may be played by men and women. In other words, there's no essential male role or essential female role, as in, "We can reduce what males do to this, or what females do to that."

If you look at modern foragers, you will find some in which there is real egalitarian cooperation between the sexes in foraging. For example, there are groups that hunt, the males and females together— not necessarily big game hunting with projectile weapons—you might envision something like net hunting in a forest, where people get into a circle, and even some of the older children can participate, and nets are used. Some people will flush out game from the bushes. Others will catch the game, and the males and females work together. They may also gather nuts together. In some societies, clearly the males are doing a great deal of hunting and are the ones providing the most calories. In other societies, the females are responsible for the vast majority of the nutrition that is brought back through gathering. So we have all sorts of situations.

This is a lesson that we should have been prepared for from primate studies. The very same point has been made through studying our closest living relatives, the great apes. We know that chimpanzees and bonobos live, in some ways, very similar lives. We know that they live in bisexual communities. Males and females live together with dependent offspring. A further commonality is that females transfer at puberty, so that the males are left living in so-called patrilines. This should all be familiar to you.

However, we cannot then say that there is a male nature. Bonobos and chimpanzees are sometimes lumped together and just called chimps because bonobos are chimp-like and they're so similar to chimpanzees, but there is no chimp-like male nature. In chimpanzees, males are aggressive. Males are entirely taken up with the dominance hierarchy and with aggressing against females. There's very little male-female cooperation. By contrast, in bonobos, the males are much less aggressive, much less caught up in dominance, and there's a great deal of co-dominance between the sexes, with females bonding together with each other to allow that co-dominance to be expressed.

We find the very same thing ethnographically around the world. So the question is, why is there such a tendency to do this behavioral sorting, to make it a simple picture in human evolution, to come out with statements such as, "Males did this and females did that?" Here is where I think we do need to appeal to the questions relating to scientific subjectivity and the larger societal patterns. The best solution may be to offer a variety of alternative behavioral scenarios that work together to try to recognize the inherent variation within a gender, within males or within females.

Here we bring back a concept that is so central to the course: variation. This is what natural selection works on, and we know that natural selection shapes behavior just as much as it does anatomy or physiology. We would expect natural selection to work on existing behavioral variation and to shape that adaptation in line with local circumstances, and that's what our models should be reflecting.

We may then try to model gender by using referential, phylogenetic, and conceptual models of non-human primates. We may go to paleoanthropological sites and model what we find out from skeletal analysis and artifactual analysis as much as we can, and then we can bring in the ethnographic analogies, but always keeping an eye on the variation that is present at every stage without making preconceptive sorts of dioramas, models or conclusions about gender.

In the next lecture, we want to return to the hominid chronological timeline that we have been building up. We want to ask about the origin of our own species, and we will devote two lectures to that. We will start by asking, when and where did modern humans first evolve?

Lecture Sixteen
Modern Human Anatomy and Behavior

Scope:

A single question forms the core of this lecture: When and where did modern human anatomy and behavior appear? The fossil record points to development of modern human anatomy by about 125,000 years ago. Modern humanity, defined anatomically, is thus quite young in evolutionary terms.

The timing of modern human *behavior* is more contentious. An earlier view converged on a radical shift in behavior at about 35,000 years ago in Europe, with the appearance of new forms of technology; symbolic representations, including art; and advances in foraging and trading. Support for this view came from the famous "cave art" sites. The beautifully rendered animal representations on the walls at Lascaux Cave, France, have long been known. Newer data from the exciting 1994 discovery of Chauvet Cave, also in France, yield an even more complete picture of the art of early *Homo sapiens*.

Based largely on two exciting archaeological African sites, scholars are reassessing the idea that a revolution in behavior can be neatly pinpointed in time at one specific region. Sophisticated tools and art predating 35,000 years ago, and found in Africa rather than Europe, indicate that scientists need to take a more global view of the origins of modern human behavior.

Outline

I.   Fully modern *Homo sapiens* differ in appearance from Neandertals and the so-called transitional forms that show a mix of *erectus-sapiens* traits.

   A.   The most dramatic changes appear in the shape of the skull. Compared to Neandertals and transitional hominids, modern humans have a high forehead, smaller brow ridges, smaller teeth, and a definite chin.

   B.   Variation can be still seen today in the modern human skull; a few populations show a more pronounced brow ridge than is the norm, for example.

C. Post-cranially, modern humans have lighter, more slender bones than Neandertals and other hominids.

II. Modern human anatomy most likely first evolved in Africa at approximately 125,00 years ago.

A. Three sites in Africa provide the most concrete evidence: Klasies River Mouth and Border Cave in South Africa, and Omo Kibish in Ethiopia. Dating of these sites, however, is not foolproof.

B. Rival sites in the quest to identify the first modern human anatomy are found in the Middle East. Two cave sites in Israel, Qafzeh and Skuhl, are the most important but probably post-date slightly the African sites.

C. Whether the African or Israeli sites turn out to be older, we can conclude that *Homo sapiens* is evolutionarily quite recent.

III. Identifying modern human behavior, and when and where it might first be found, is an order of magnitude more difficult than the search for the first modern anatomy.

A. Typically, by the term *modern behavior*, biological anthropologists refer to a cluster of innovations relating to technology, art and other symbolic representation, and advances in foraging and trading.

B. Biological anthropologists initially traced these behavioral innovations to Western Europe, suggesting that they appeared there at about 35,000 years ago. In this view, there was a great leap forward in human behavior in a single time and place.

1. So-called Upper Paleolithic tools in Europe at this time show fine workmanship in wood, bone, and antler.

2. Breathtaking examples of art, only seen after 30,000 years ago, have long been known from such caves as Lascaux in France. In 1994, Chauvet Cave was discovered, also in France, yielding amazing new clues to hominid art. Portable art is also associated with the Upper Paleolithic in Europe.

3. These advances and others in hunting and long-distance exchange of objects look wholly different from anything produced by Neandertals, or other hominids, according to many scholars.

C. Recently, evidence suggests that instead of a sudden behavioral revolution in Europe, modern human behavior may have appeared more gradually and in a more distributed way around the globe.

1. Although it seems clear that *Homo sapiens* is set apart from other hominids behaviorally, the early focus on a specific behavioral revolution may be, in part, the result of a Eurocentric bias. Africa may once again be implicated in some "firsts" in human evolution, as it has been so often.

2. New excavations at two African modern-human sites, Katanda in Zaire and Blombos Cave in South Africa, are forcing reevaluations of the appearance of sophisticated modern technology. Bone, for example, appears to be very finely worked at these sites. These sites significantly predate the supposed European behavioral revolution.

3. Rock art in Namibia and other places in Africa date to approximately the same time periods as the French caves.

IV. In sum, it appears that modern human anatomy evolved before the cluster of traits that we refer to as modern human behavior. However, the timing for appearance of modern human behavior has shifted appreciably in just the last few decades. The old idea that Africa was the home of early human evolution but that modern human behavior evolved in Europe is now suspect.

Essential Reading:

Jurmain et al., *Introduction to Physical Anthropology*, chapter 13, second half.

Questions to Consider:

1. What questions would arise for paleoanthropology if the Israeli *Homo sapiens* sites are found to predate the sites in Africa?

2. Two sites excavated in the 1990s are significantly altering our understanding of the origins of modern human behavior. What are the main new findings at Chauvet Cave in France and Blombos Cave in South Africa?

Lecture Sixteen—Transcript
Modern Human Anatomy and Behavior

Let's continue now with our hominid chronology because we still must account for the emergence of our own species, *Homo sapiens*; and in this lecture, we will talk about both the anatomy and the behavior of *Homo sapiens* as it first evolved. If you line up a Neandertal skull or skeleton and put it next to a *Homo sapiens* skull and skeleton, there are quite striking differences.

We'll start with the skull. There are four traits of the *Homo sapiens* skull that set it apart immediately from what we would see looking at a Neandertal skull. First of all, the high forehead: we have this vertical—domed, if you will—forehead that looks immediately different from the low, sloping nature of the Neandertal forehead. Secondly, we have either greatly reduced or nonexistent brow ridges, that bar of bone over the eyes. Third, we also have smaller teeth; and fourth, related to number three, a definite chin. I'm referring to "we" because we're *Homo sapiens*, but I'm talking about traits that extend through the entire time period, from the first *Homo sapiens* and continuing now through the present day.

People often ask, "Why a chin? Why would a chin appear in the hominid line with *Homo sapiens* at this particular time?" It seems as if there's a reconfiguration of the lower jaw that may well reflect relaxed selection pressures on the teeth. The teeth, we know, are getting smaller, and apparently they were being used now for things like chewing and eating rather than for things that they might have been used for before, as an aid to technology. The Neandertals' big incisors, for example, have led anthropologists to speculate that they used their teeth as tools; and as the toolkit improved with *Homo sapiens*, it seems likely that the teeth were used less and less often as tools and more and more often for just feeding, leading to this reconfiguration of the lower jaw.

It is true, nonetheless, that despite the pattern of these four characteristics, we still see a lot of variation within modern human populations. To give you just one example, there are populations today that do show more pronounced brow ridges than are typical. The Australian aborigines would be a good illustration of this. Australian aborigines are full modern, fully sapient, just like any other population, but they have retained a slightly pronounced brow ridge. That is just a typical example of what we call *intra-specific variation*, within one species.

What about below the neck then, making this comparison between hominids and modern humans? Post-cranially, modern humans have a lighter, slender skeleton that is less robust and less heavy, not the kind of adaptation for cold that we see in Neandertals and not the strength that we see in the Neandertals, so we have a move away from a robust adaptation.

Modern human anatomy, as far as we know now, appeared in the fossil record at about 125,000 years ago, and the place that this first appeared seems to be Africa. This is going to be our working hypothesis for this lecture. There are three sites in Africa that provide the best evidence in support of this claim. Two are cave sites in South Africa. One is called Klasies River Mouth, and one is called Border Cave. The third site is in East Africa in Ethiopia, and it is called Omo Kibish. All of these have skeletons that are without a doubt modern. The characteristics are there; there's no dispute.

What does tend to be disputed is the date. The best date is around 125,000; but unfortunately, it is not extremely precise. In other words, there is a large waffle factor around this date, a plus or minus accuracy range. It might be true; it might be a little bit old or it might be a little bit young as an estimate of when these people actually lived.

Klasies River Mouth is a site that I would very much like to visit. I have not been able to go to South Africa, but it is particularly interesting. This is a site showing that early modern humans lived on the South African seacoast. They set up their living area between the actual cave and a large dune that is apparently quite old that would have sheltered them from the winds coming in off of the water. Paleoanthropologists have been able to analyze remains of diets that have been found there, and have shown that these people were very efficient extractors of seafood from this area. We know that these early *Homo sapiens* ate clams, mussels, and also larger creatures as well, including penguins and seals.

Our working hypothesis is in place, but there is a rival to it, and the rival hypothesis looks at sites of early *Homo sapiens* in the Middle East, specifically in Israel, and suggests that these might be as old as the three sites that I've just talked to you about. To give some specifics, we can work from two examples in Israel. There are two sites, Skuhl and Qafzeh, which have been dated to right around 100,000 years ago.

Obviously, that estimate is younger, more recent than the African sites; but when you factor in that plus or minus, the fact that the dates could be off one way or the other, they're pretty close for fine evolutionary modeling. So there is a problematic nature of trying to come up with a sequence of whether the African sites were first or the Israeli sites were first; but probably the African sites are, in fact, oldest.

Whatever turns out to be the case, we can say with a great deal of confidence that *Homo sapiens* is a young species. Let's consider the whole time sweep of this course. At 65 million years ago, we had an ancestral population of mammals that began to evolve in the direction of primates. Only at seven million years ago do we have a form that appears to be the first hominid, the first example on the hominid lineage with a bipedal creature. At 2.4 million years ago, we get a hominid in our own genus, the genus *Homo*. That is, of course, *Homo habilis*, and we have to move down the time scale all the way to 125,000 years ago before we get to us. This is quite recent when we talk about evolutionary time.

So much for human anatomy. What we really are interested in is the origins of modern behavior, because being modern is about more than having a high forehead or a chin. We want to understand what types of behavioral advances were tied up in this change in evolutionary time.

The first problem comes in by even defining what could be meant by modern behavior. Typically, biological anthropologists refer to a cluster of innovations. As you might expect, technology would be included—advances in stone tool and other types of tool technology, as well—but it goes beyond technology to bring in the first appearance of art. The idea that there is now trading happening over some fairly long distances, and a strong interest in reconstructing symbolic representation. The idea that *Homo sapiens*, more than any other hominid—and possibly exclusively—was able to rely on symbolic representation of, let's say, images, and we'll talk more about that in just a minute.

As we have done before, we're not going to worry so much about the great variety in definitions, but we're going to look at some of the best evidence and some of the patterns that we can find for modern human beings. For quite a long time, biological anthropologists traced modern human behavior to a particular place and a particular time. That place was Western Europe, and the time was right around 35,000 years ago.

This was given a nickname. This was called a *behavioral revolution*, or more informally, the "great leap forward" that happened at 35,000 years ago. Everything was supposed to have made a relatively sudden change, so that, in fact, we have to look at one part of the world to understand how we really became human, on this view.

What evidence was there for such a pinpointing of modern human behavior in time and space? Let's start with the technology. The so-called Upper Paleolithic tools that appear in Europe at this time are key. Upper Paleolithic is just a designation of a particular time period, and it refers to right around 35,000 years ago in Western Europe, and the tools that are found at this time are amazingly well crafted. They are reflective of very precise, very decorative craftsmanship. So the tools, while for the most part are functional, some are actually decorative and artistic to the exclusion of function.

For example, wood, bone and antler are now worked and used as tools as much as stone actually is, and we don't have that from before. There are burin tools [chisel-like] that are actually used to make other tools. In other word, the burins work the wood, the bone and the antler, and produce other tools from there. We have drilling tools that were used to drill holes. We can find ancient shells with holes drilled in them, and the tools that apparently were used to make those holes. So something new is going on here in terms of innovation, decoration and craftsmanship.

A very important area of research has been tied up with the appearance art, with modern *Homo sapiens*. There are just spectacular examples of art from Western Europe, and we'll start off talking about cave paintings. I want to spend a little while talking about them because they're so illustrative of what I'm talking about, and they're so much fun to talk about, as well. The cave art tends to be dated to right around 30,000 years ago or after, or more recently than that. We've known about this cave art for a while.

I suspect many of you have heard of Lascaux Cave in France, which has been studied for many decades. Particularly famous is a room called the Great Hall of Bulls. There are animal representations, animal paintings in color all over this room, and I should tell you before we go further that the date for this room and the cave altogether is 17,000 years ago, and we are dealing with France now. When you walk into the Great Hall of Bulls, or any other room in this cave, what strikes you immediately is the color—there's red and black and other colors that are painted on the walls—and the real artistic elegance of the animal paintings that you see.

When I was first being taught about this topic, my teacher told me, "Don't think about this as being some incipient form of art, some precursor to art or maybe even something in between a child's drawing and an adult's drawing. No, this is full artistic competence at work." The animal paintings are realistic. They really look like the bison or the deer or whatever is depicted. Furthermore, if there's a natural feature in the cave, it was often incorporated into the paintings. Let's say there's a very small outcropping coming out of the cave wall, a sort of bulge on the cave wall. That might have been incorporated as a shoulder or a rippling muscle. So clearly, there was full art at this time period.

It's worth learning a little bit more about Lascaux, because it has quite a lot to tell us about prehistory. Basically, in the art that's on the walls, there are three themes represented: animals, humans and what are called *signs*, and I'll be defining that for you in a minute. The animal representations are far and away the most dominant. There are approximately 600 animal representations on these cave walls. A full quarter of them are horses. There's a great lot of one particular species. Bison is the next most popular, and there are a few other species, as well. As I mentioned, you need to be thinking of animals that we can instantly identify and have no problem knowing what they are.

The second category is human representation. Quite intriguingly, there is simply one example in this category. In all of Lascaux Cave, in all of the rooms, there is one human figure; and unlike what we have been talking about with the animal representations, this human figure is quite stylized. That is, it is not realistic looking at all. It is almost at the level of a stick figure, a drawn outline, something that a child might do, which is very intriguing if we start to think about meanings, which we'll come back to in a minute.

The third category, that has been called *signs*, includes things like dots, curves and lines—basically, sort of geometric types of things that aren't representations of living creatures. So this has been a source of interest and excitement for paleoanthropologists for quite a long time.

I mentioned, when you walk into the Hall of Bulls—and I should explain that I have not been there; I hope to go—for a long time, it was possible for anyone to walk into Lascaux Cave and view these cave paintings. The country of France was quite proud of this and allowed people to go in and see them. Right about 1955 it became clear that the cave walls and the paintings were deteriorating because of the large amount of carbon dioxide that people were exhaling as they went through, and this was not a tenable situation. One doesn't want to take 17,000-year-old cave paintings and have them deteriorating or even destroyed.

By 1963, the cave was closed. It just became clear that the paintings could not withstand the tourism. I'm happy to say that the paintings have been restored simply by the passage of time and not having all that carbon dioxide around. They're back to their initial freshness and vitality.

The country of France also made an interesting decision. They decided to reproduce the full, life-size model, the Hall of Bulls, and another room from Lascaux cave and set it up as what's called Lascaux II, and this is a place people can go. This is a life-like replica of the very same cave, with everything made just the way that it appears to be in the original, so that again, these small outcroppings on the cave walls are incorporated into the art, and everything is exactly the same.

So if you happen to be going to France, this is a place that you might consider visiting. If you're not getting to go to France any time soon—as I am not—you might want to try a virtual visit. If you have access to the Internet and you're comfortable with search engines, simply typing in "Lascaux Cave" can lead you to a beautiful virtual tour where these images at the Hall of Bulls and elsewhere are visible to you.

I don't mean to focus on Lascaux to the exclusion of other caves. We know of others in Italy and in Spain, as well. There are quite a lot of caves in this Western European area. Furthermore, people are still discovering such caves. The most recent truly amazing discovery was in 1994. There was a man called Chauvet who was walking on a hiking trail and had known about a cave that was in this particular area for some time, but noticed some air coming up from the cave in a way that he hadn't noticed before and was intrigued by. He collected two friends. They were all quite comfortable with cave exploration and began to search for an opening that had not been known about but that might account for these air currents, and they did find a hidden opening and push their way through.

They found, not only a great big chamber when they entered, but also a network of rooms beyond that. Of course, it was dark in there. They had lights. They were able to see a little bit. One of them looked up and saw the depiction of a mammoth on the cave wall in red ochre, and at that point they knew clearly they had quite a discovery. Since 1994, there has been ongoing analysis and research at the cave, which is called Chauvet Cave.

Some aspects of this cave are quite different than what we saw in the discussion of Lascaux Cave. For example, there are still many animal depictions and animal representations, and they are still exquisite. They're just beautiful and elegant, but they tend to be of different types of animals. For example, what's depicted here includes rhino, lion and bear, animals that are absent from Lascaux, and they are also animals that tend not to be hunted as much as, say, horses and deer. There are, in fact, three animals depicted on the cave walls at Chauvet that have never been seen in any other cave at all: panther, hyena and owl—quite intriguing. There are also a lot of human hands—in other words, the image of hands—around the cave at Chauvet.

In addition to the cave paintings that I've been describing to you at these two French sites, we know of other types of art from this time period in Western Europe, and this other type of art can be summarized by the label "portable art": things that are much smaller and can be carried from place to place. Probably the most famous portable art in the Upper Paleolithic time period are the Venus figurines. These are small statues of women, and they tend to come in two types.

One is highly stylized—again, not realistic. The facial features and even the hair are very blurry. They're not clear at all, but what get very exaggerated are areas of breasts, the hips and the buttocks— huge amounts of fat deposits on these areas. This led to the idea that has become quite famous that these Venus figurines might be some kind of a fertility cult.

I don't know about that. There are other hypotheses as well, and we need to keep in mind that some Venus figurines are quite realistic and do not have fat deposits depicted on them, so here we're not sure what is going on, but there are lots of these statues. There are also engravings; for example, piece of stone or bone with decorations on them. This is important to keep in mind, and should not be overshadowed entirely by the cave art.

So these kinds of advances that we're talking about are, without a doubt, different than anything that transitional hominids or Neandertals have produced, at least to our knowledge, unless there's a surprise in store for us. We can then come to the conclusion that there's a new level of symbolic representation with *Homo sapiens*. Of course, the one question that I haven't tackled so far is, what do all these cave paintings mean, and what do all the engravings mean? This is what we would truly like to know, but we run up against the same old problem: how do we interpret from way back in prehistory?

As you would also not be surprised to hear, there's been no shortage of theorizing. Let's take the animal depictions at Chauvet and Lascaux for our example. Could it be that this is a type of hunting magic or hunting ritual? In other words, for the hunters that go out and try to take down bison or horses, if you put the image on the cave wall, could that somehow be an attempt to gain power or control over the animal? Other suggestions have been that maybe teaching was involved. For example, adolescents who are about to start hunting might be taught about the species.

But clearly, there is more going on than just hunting, since at Chauvet, we have those rare depictions of the lion, the rhino, the owl and the panther, and so on. I have always wondered myself if it couldn't just be art for pleasure's sake? Does there have to be a particular function that we need to figure out for this art? Scholars who know more than I about art are hard at work on this question.

Let's return to the question of the behavioral revolution in Western Europe. What we have learned so far is that there *was* reason to suggest such a sudden, abrupt revolution, by all the tools and the art that we know of from this place and this time. However, recent evidence suggests that the conclusion of the "great leap forward" may well have been too hasty. In fact, modern human behavior may have appeared in a more distributed way around the globe, and more gradually.

There's an interesting question that is hidden behind what I've just said. The question can be formed as follows: Has there been a Eurocentric bias to our study of the emergence of modern behavior? That is, have we been looking in Europe because we expected Europe to be the home of symbolization, innovation, and all of the things that we've been talking about? Is it possible that scholars who live and work in Europe thought, "Yes, Africa is a fine home for the early stages of human evolution, but when we really become human and our behavior takes on the added significance and symbolization that we're talking about, we better look in Europe"?

I don't know, but what I do know is that new excavations in Africa are very compelling to mount a counter-proposal to the behavioral revolution idea, and we need to talk about two sites in particular in this context. The first is called Katanda, and it's found in the Democratic Republic of Congo, formerly Zaire—most people know the country as Zaire—and Blombos Cave in South Africa. Both places show extremely fine craftsmanship of tools, particularly focusing on bone.

Let's take up first the case of Katanda. There are two American archaeologists who deserve credit for the excavation at this site: Alison Brooks and John Yellen. What they have found are finely worked bone harpoon points. As I indicated, they're beautifully crafted; but, what the real surprise turned out to be was the date. Between 80- and 90,000 years ago, in Africa, we have the very same type of elegant tools that we were claiming should only appear in Western Europe at 35,000 years ago.

When Katanda was the single example in Africa, it was fairly easy to dismiss it or to say, "Who knows about those dates?," or to say, "This is a single example." We are learning from Blombos Cave in South Africa that it is not the only example. Christopher Henshilwood has been telling us about excavations at Blombos for just a few years now, and quite recently has made a new, exciting announcement. He has found a piece of red ochre—red stone—two pieces in fact, with triangles and lines on them that are quite clearly inscribed and engraved; and again, what is important is the date: 77,000 years ago.

This is not the only piece of information from Blombos. In fact, he had published earlier about bone tools that are finely worked, and they are dated to 70,000 years ago. In this case, we're talking about projectile points that have been made from bone. So when you put together the evidence from Blombos with the evidence from Katanda, at the very least you have a strong reason to question the human behavioral revolution as being centered in one time and one place.

You might ask, "That may work for technology, but what about art?" One poll that I'd be very interested to take—and I think I will do this when I teach this course next at William and Mary—is to ask this question of students, "How many of you have heard of the cave paintings at Lascaux in France?" And we'll get a certain percentage answer, and then ask, "How many of you have heard about the rock art at Apollo 11 Cave in Namibia in Southern Africa?" I can predict for you that the percentage for that second question will be lower than the percentage for the first.

Namibian cave art is not something that is as well known as the Western European cave art. We do find in Africa rock paintings that are just in the same art time period that we've been talking about for Western Europe. For example, the Apollo 11 Cave has charcoal and red and white animals that are depicted just as elegantly as we do in Western Europe—not as many of them—but one thing that's quite surprising is the date: 27,000 years ago. So 10,000 years before *Homo sapiens* were making Lascaux, they were living in Namibia and making these rock art drawings. So it seems clear that *Homo sapiens* are set apart from any creatures that came before, whether we talk about technology, or art, or basically clump all of this together into talking about symbolic innovation. We also remember from some of these examples—and from what we talked about earlier—that *Homo sapiens* is doing a different kind of hunting now. There is not the need to do what Neandertals did—close-quarter hunting—or perhaps what transitional hominids did—of always stampeding animals off of cliffs—rather, projectiles such as the bow and arrow, the spear-thrower, harpoon points and other projectiles are all in use now, so there's no question about that.

What we have to ask is whether we have been restricting ourselves too much by looking only in Western Europe at what *Homo sapiens* was doing. So we need to ask new questions. It is possible that Africa may be implicated one again, as it has been so many times before, in some firsts, now talking about behavioral innovation with *Homo sapiens*.

Let's sum up this lecture. It appears that modern human anatomy did evolve before what we want to call modern human behavior. This is an interesting fact in itself. Whether we look at Katanda at 80- or 90,000 years ago, or we look at the art in Western Europe at 30,000 years ago, that seems to have happened more recently than when we see the skeletal and skull changes as being, which can be dated to 125,000 years ago. Remember that the anatomical changes are a slenderizing, if you will, of the skeleton, the high forehead, the reconfiguration of the face, and the loss of the brow ridges in the skull. All of that comes about first; and as far as we are able to tell, the behavioral innovations come later.

I always want to say that there should be a qualification in there, because dates change and we may find new things. The old idea, that Africa was the home of early human evolution but that modern human behavior evolved in Europe, is now suspect.

One area of symbolic representation that I did not touch on in this lecture deserves a quick mention here at the end, and that is language. I have left out talking about the evolution of speech and the evolution of language because I am going to devote an entire lecture to that topic. Certainly, speech and language counts as an example of symbolization, and we will tackle that in Lecture Eighteen.

Before we do that though, we have more work to do on the topic of origins of *Homo sapiens*. We have to ask now, from where did *Homo sapiens* emerge? From what other populations did they evolve, and how did it come to be that at a certain point in human evolutionary history, *Homo sapiens* became the sole hominid on Earth? So stay tuned for the next lecture.

Lecture Seventeen
On the Origins of *Homo sapiens*

Scope:

We know that *Homo sapiens* is a young species, in evolutionary terms; we humans are no older than 125,000 years anatomically, with modern behavior appearing even more recently than that. But from which hominid populations did *Homo sapiens* evolve? And at what point did modern humans become the sole hominid on Earth?

Homo sapiens likely evolved from transitional hominid populations living between 400,000 and 200,000 years ago; by about 30,000 years ago, our species was the only hominid alive on Earth. Two major models try to explain modern human origins. Scientists who support the *Out-of-Africa replacement* model suggest that *Homo sapiens* developed first in Africa, then migrated out across the world, replacing all other hominid populations as they went. Those who support the rival *multiregional* model insist that *Homo sapiens* evolved locally on three continents, each regional population responding to local selection pressures.

Each model produces different predictions. To evaluate these differentially, three sources of information can be used. Hominid sites and specific fossils can be compared across regions of the world. Evolutionary theory allows assessment of more likely and less likely scenarios of evolutionary change. Finally, DNA can be analyzed to identify pathways of genetic changes over time.

At this point in the course, it is likely no surprise to learn that biological anthropologists can reach no consensus on which model to support. It is even possible that an intermediate sort of model, combining elements of both the Out-of-Africa and multiregional models, might be the best candidate for explaining modern human origins.

Outline

I.   Modern humans originated no earlier than about 125,000 years ago. Between that time and 30,000 years ago, *Homo sapiens* shared the Earth with Neandertals. Could our species have evolved from Neandertals?

A. Given that Neandertals and modern humans evolved at about the same time, it is unlikely that Neandertals gave rise to modern humans. Rather, we can think of the two species as co-inhabiting certain areas at certain times.

    1. Neandertals and modern humans occupied the same general region of the Middle East between about 90,000 and 60,000 years ago. Biological anthropologists have no sense of whether the two species directly met.

    2. Neandertals and modern humans not only occupied the same regions of Western Europe at about 40,000 years ago, but biological anthropologists are fairly sure that the two species met and competed for resources.

B. Neandertals and modern humans may have both arisen from the same or similar earlier hominid populations, then adapted in different directions to different selection pressures.

    1. A plausible hypothesis is that *Homo erectus* evolved into transitional hominids marked by a mix of *erectus-sapiens* characteristics. Populations lived in Africa, Asia, and Europe between 400,000 and 130,000 years ago.

    2. Some populations evolved in the direction of modern *Homo sapiens*, whereas others did not.

II. The *Out-of-Africa replacement* hypothesis posits that all the evolutionary "action" in modern human origins occurred in Africa. Modern forms then spread out through the Old World, replacing all other hominid populations.

    A. Modern humans first evolved in Africa, as evidenced by the sites of Klasies River Mouth, Border Cave, and Omo.

    B. As hominids migrated north out of Africa, they encountered other hominid populations and replaced them but without interbreeding.

III. The *multiregional* hypothesis posits that evolution of modern humans occurred on three continents.

    A. Gradual evolution in Africa, Asia, and Europe accounts for the origins of modern humans in this perspective.

    B. Gene flow among populations on these three continents prevented speciation from occurring.

C. Replacement of one hominid population by another did not occur; rather, *Homo erectus* and other hominids evolved locally and gradually into *Homo sapiens.*

IV. Multiple sources of evidence can be brought to bear in testing these two models.

    A. Precise dating of archaeological sites is crucial; if the African *Homo sapiens* sites are not, in fact, the earliest, then the Out-of-Africa position is weakened.

    B. Comparison of fossil anatomy from different regions produces a mixed picture.

        1. In some regions, for example, in Asia, there seems to be clear evidence of local continuity. That is, certain features can be traced across long periods of time within a certain region (but not across regions). This fact supports the multiregional model.

        2. On the other hand, a corollary of the multiregional model is that in Europe, Neandertals evolved into modern humans. As we have seen, this situation seems unlikely.

    C. At least one reading of evolutionary theory appears to support the Out-of-Africa model. Stephen Jay Gould says that the multiregional model is very unlikely because it requires disparate populations to evolve in the same direction, despite variant local selection pressures.

    D. Out-of-Africa theorists have claimed that DNA analysis supports their case. A variety of methods have been attempted, most famously the one involving "mitochondrial Eve."

        1. Mitochondrial DNA (mtDNA) is a subtype of DNA inherited only through the maternal line. Changes in mtDNA come about only through mutation and, thus, can be used to trace ancestry.

        2. A study of modern variation in women's mtDNA showed that the greatest variation exists in Africa, implying that African people evolved first. It was even deduced that the first African, the so-called mitochondrial Eve, lived in Africa at about 200,000 years ago.

3. Subsequent genetic tests cast doubts on the precise methods used to reach the conclusion about mitochondrial Eve. In any case, skeptics, especially those who espouse the multiregional model, say it is misleading to imply that one specific modern human female was the mother of us all.

V. A possible solution in the stalemate between the two models of modern human origins is to embrace an intermediate model, which is called the *partial replacement model*.

   A. In this third model, *Homo sapiens* did migrate north from Africa, where they first originated.

   B. Along the way, these individuals hybridized to some degree with local hominid populations. Replacement, thus, occurred gradually.

VI. Returning to a familiar refrain, we can sum up by saying that biological anthropology has produced good, solid, testable models about the nature of modern human origins; we now await more data to differentiate among them.

Essential Reading:

Jurmain et al., *Introduction to Physical Anthropology*, chapter 13, first half.

Sykes, *The Seven Daughters of Eve.*

Questions to Consider:

1. What evidence do you believe would be most helpful in nailing down either the Out-of-Africa or multiregional model?

2. Why is mtDNA more useful in tracing ancient ancestries than is regular (nuclear) DNA?

Lecture Seventeen—Transcript
On the Origins of *Homo sapiens*

Having just considered the origins of anatomy and behavior in modern *Homo sapiens*, we are now going to shift to a different but related question. From which hominid populations did *Homo sapiens* evolve? Our starting point is one central fact, and that is the extreme overlap in time between *Homo sapiens* and *Homo neandertalensis*. Remember that our starting point for Neandertals is 130,000 years ago; and equally significantly, our starting point for *Homo sapiens* is 125,000 years ago. Therefore, the two species had a great deal of time in which they lived near each other in the same geographic regions at the same time.

Biological anthropologists are not always certain about the kind, or type, or even fact of interaction between these two species; but this key fact of the overlapping time tells us right away that it is unlikely that modern *Homo sapiens* evolved from Neandertals. If we have these parallel lines or parallel species, it's unlikely that Neandertals would have given rise to modern humans.

Let's look at this time period of overlap and talk about two different geographic locations. We'll start in the Middle East. We know that Neandertals and modern humans occupied the same general regions of the Middle East between about 90,000 and 60,000 years ago. This was a very busy place during that time period. One archaeologist refers to this area as a type of central bus station, with hominids and modern humans moving in and moving out. You will recall that we know of good dates: Qafzeh and Skuhl, in Israel for modern humans at around 100,000 years ago. Let's stick with the same country of Israel and ask what type of occupation we have evidence for, for the Neandertals.

There are two sites that we can point to. One is called Tabun, and one is called Kebara. Tabun is dated to about 110,000 years ago; Kebara is dated to about 60,000 years ago. So right there, you have a 50,000-year—at least—time span for Neandertals during the time that we have modern humans living in the area. So, parallel lengthy occupations. But there is not good evidence to suggest whether these two species actually met. There's nothing in the fossil record that tells us either yes or no, there was direct interaction, so we can only speculate about that.

The situation is a little bit different if we leap ahead in time to around 40- to 35,000 years ago, and we shift geographic location to Western Europe. Here, biological anthropologists are quite sure that the two species did interact. Their locations were quite close, and there's some evidence of the same area being occupied very tightly, very close in, with different sites, some for Neandertals and some for humans.

You'll recall from a previous lecture that we talked about Chauvet Cave in France, with very good evidence of spectacular art by *Homo sapiens* dated to right around 30,000 years ago. In France also, we have Neandertal sites dated to the very same time period. We have bones of Neandertals and *Homo sapiens*, and artifacts of both, in a tightly enclosed area, and the key fact is that by around 30,000 years ago, just at the time period of ascendancy, if you will, of *Homo sapiens*, we have disappearance of Neandertals, extinction of Neandertals, from the fossil record.

It may be closer to 28,000 than 30—this is debated now—but right around that time period; and it seems quite clear that this extinction of the Neandertals was due to competition with modern humans. We don't mean to imply that there was lethal violence or outright hand-to-hand combat here. Competition, in evolutionary terms, refers to reproductive success, and different types of competition can account for that. So, we may simply be talking about resource out-competition by modern humans against the Neandertals.

The Neandertals and the modern humans may have both arisen from the same hominid population and then adapted in different directions due to different selection pressures early on in their parallel lineages. A plausible hypothesis takes as its starting point, *Homo erectus*, which would then have evolved into transitional hominids with the *erectus-sapiens* mix, and then different populations moving in different directions. We know that we have all of these varied populations between 400,000 and 130,000 years ago, and then the Neandertal lineage and the modern human lineage, so some populations evolved in the direction of modern *Homo sapiens*, and some did not. This is about as specific as we can get in this fuzzy area of ancestry, as we talked about last time.

What we want to talk about are some very sharply drawn models of the origins of *Homo sapiens*. We are at the stage where we have very clear models to test, and we're working on getting enough evidence to test them. So what I want to talk about for a while is what the models predict and how the evidence we do have fits into the testing of the models, and we'll see that we are awaiting more evidence, as well. So the question before us, again: Where did *Homo sapiens* come from?

The first model we want to consider takes the term the *Out-of-Africa replacement* model. Here there's a claim that all of the evolutionary action at this point in time for the origins of modern humans occurred in Africa, that African sites are the oldest, and that modern forms spread out from this one particular place and then moved through the rest of the world. Clearly, when modern humans moved through other parts of the world, they would have encountered other earlier hominid populations, and this particular model says that replacement occurred. That is, modern *Homo sapiens* out-competed everybody else without interbreeding with them. That is a key component. There was no hybridization, but rather just total out-competition and total domination by modern *Homo sapiens*.

So what evidence is there? For the claim being focused on Africa, we need to return to those sites that we have already talked about, particularly in Southern Africa: Klasies River Mouth and Border Cave, and also the site in East Africa, in Ethiopia, of Omo. The early dates that have been provisionally assigned to these sites are key, because they back up the idea of origins in Africa. We also want to look at this claim of no interbreeding, and we'll see later that we can talk about some genetic data in this regard.

There are people who are quite convinced that this model is correct and stake their reputations and careers on it, but there is an extremely heated response to this. In fact, this is a type of question—if you go to anthropology conferences or paleoanthropology meetings—that guarantees a conference session being essentially sold out, standing room only. If you get the Out-of-Africa people debating with the other side, it's really very exciting and very heated.

The other side is called the *multiregional* model. The multiregionalists reject the idea that the center of evolutionary action is in Africa. They suggest origins can be found of modern humans on three continents, and you'll know which ones: Africa, Europe and Asia. The idea is that there was gradual evolution in all of these places that can account for modern humans. We might want to call this *in situ* evolution. In other words, wherever earlier hominid populations exist, they slowly and gradually develop towards modernity in response to local selection pressures.

If you think back to earlier lectures, you might have a question, and that is, if you're dealing with three different locations, you know that if there had been reproductive isolation—each population, broadly speaking, on a continent evolving on its own—there would have been speciation. We would have ended up with three different types of humans of species, and that didn't happen.

So, a key fact in the multiregional model is that gene flow had to occur between and among these populations across the continents simply to prevent speciation from occurring. Replacement of one hominid population by another did not occur, on this account. *Homo erectus*, wherever it was found, developed slowly through the transitional hominids into modern humans.

There is even a claim, which follows sort of naturally, that Neandertals, where they were found, or at least the earlier part of the Neandertal lineage, would also have evolved *in situ* to modern humans. This does tend to be a sticking point, as you can see, given what I started the lecture with, by saying there's so much overlap in time. So we have again, as I've said, a choice: two models with different predictions. Can we test them? That's what the real prize would be, to take the evidence and test the models.

To a certain extent, yes. We can bring three major sources of data to bear on testing these models. You can look at the sites and the fossils found at them, the skeletons and skulls and what they tell us; you can use evolutionary theory to assess the logic of the models and you can use genetics. We have talked on and off about the fact that a complementary source of data to the bones are the molecules, the genes.

Let's start with the sites and the fossils. Precise dating of sites is crucial here. If the African sites—Klasies River, Border Cave, and Omo—are not actually the oldest ones, the Out-of-Africa replacement model is significantly weakened. If it turns out that Qafzeh and Skuhl in Israel do tend to be older, in the dates in terms of the plus and minus problem that we had talked about before, the range of dates, then you've got a problem. So dating is going to be the key underpinning of this part of the Out-of-Africa model.

What about the fossils themselves? What do the fossil anatomies have to say? The multiregional modelers depend very heavily on one key fact that is derived from comparative anatomy, and we can call this *local continuity in anatomical features*. The idea here is that if you look in any given continental region, you should see continuity of the features in the face and the skeleton in that region through time, but not find that continuity in another region. So it's within-region continuity, not across-region continuity, and in some places we do see this.

A good example comes from Asia. Let's start at *Homo erectus*. We know already that there's a very long occupation of Asia by *Homo erectus*. In the early skulls and throughout the time period, there's a certain type of incisor that is characteristic of *Homo erectus*, and I'm referring here to the front teeth. There's a certain shape, a shovel-shaped incisor, it's called, and that trait continues in Asia from *Homo erectus*, through the transitional hominids, and into the modern day, but it is not found in Africa and Europe.

The multiregional modelers say, "Bingo, exactly. This is what we would expect to find." They say, in fact, if the Out-of-Africa modelers were correct, you'd expect to find at the time of migration north from Africa—at the time of the supposed replacement—you'd get a break in the sequence of shovel-shaped incisors, because remember, the Out-of-Africa modelers say that there's no interbreeding, so you would have replacement of the Asian characteristics by the African characteristics. It doesn't happen.

However, the news is not all good for the multiregional model, because a corollary of this model is that in Europe, Neandertals should have evolved into modern humans, and we see that that just doesn't work. It doesn't work with the time period. It doesn't work with the anatomy. There are sharp differences there. So once again, the Neandertal and modern human parallel lineage problem comes back to haunt the multiregional people.

Let's move to our second source of data: that is, understanding evolutionary theory and bringing it to bear on the problem. At least one reading of evolutionary theory supports the Out-of-Africa model, and it's a very good reading because it's by Stephen Jay Gould, a theorist we have relied upon before in this course. Stephen Jay Gould says that the multiregional model is very unlikely. After all, what it's asking us to believe is that disparate, separate populations would have evolved in the same direction despite being subject to different local selection pressures, and he asks, that's not really the way evolution works, is it?

After all, he says, are there any models that start out with a kind of proto-rat—he's talking about a rodent, a mammal here—in some parts of the world, and these separate populations all march in lockstep from proto-ratitude to being true rats? He says no, there are no such models. Why? Because nobody, according to Gould, is interested in positing the inevitability of evolution of rats.

What he's really saying here is that our human vanity is wrapped up in the multiregional model, that we want to see this inevitable progression, wherever hominids lived, towards humanity. We don't want to think of contingency actually being part of our evolution. By contingency, he means things happened a certain way, but they might well have happened a different way. They happened a certain way in Africa, Gould says, supporting the Out-of-Africa model.

What he believes—believed, because he's died—is that, in fact, the factors that we can bring to bear show that whatever pressures happened in Africa started off the modern human line—got us going, essentially—and then we did replace hominids elsewhere. What's useful about this is that it does take us out of looking only at hominids and humans, and it brings other animals, the evolutionary record of other animals and evolutionary theory into the perspective, so I think that it's worth considering.

Lastly, the genetic evidence. For a long time, the Out-of-Africa theorists relied very heavily on a specific type of DNA analysis to support their claims. A variety of methods had been attempted, but one became quite well known, and it's one that you've probably heard of in some form. It involves the so-called *mitochondrial Eve*.

In order to understand who mitochondrial Eve was supposed to be, we need to understand what mitochondrial DNA is. Mitochondrial DNA, which is abbreviated mtDNA conventionally, is a sub-type of DNA that's inherited only through the maternal line, so immediately you'll know this is different. Normally, if you reflect upon it, you can think that your own DNA is a mix of what you get from your mother and what you get from your father.

Not so with mtDNA. It's strictly maternally inherited, and what that means then, is that changes in mtDNA through a particular family or lineage come about through only one source, and that source is mutation. Those are the two things you need to know about mtDNA: maternal inheritance and changes through mutation only. The combination of these factors means that we can use mtDNA to trace ancestry back in time, at least theoretically.

A study was done in the early 1990s that collected mtDNA samples from modern living women around the globe. These women donated these samples from all different continents, and the mtDNA samples were compared in the laboratory. The key finding is that the greatest variation in mtDNA was found among the women living in Africa. This implied to the researchers that African people had evolved first.

Why? Because the diversity is a code for saying that there were more mutations, and it takes time to accumulate mutations. So we can think of an equation here: more mutations equal more evolutionary time. This was a pretty robust finding, so this is another way to say that it seems like modern humans might have originated in Africa.

Of course, the researchers wanted also to come up with a specific time of origin for all of this mtDNA diversity, and they did that and deduced that the first African woman who was responsible for all of this mtDNA diversity in the modern world would have lived about 200,000 years ago, and she was nicknamed "mitochondrial Eve."

The process by which the date is derived is very similar to the one that we talked about quite a few lectures ago when we talked about deriving a time at which the common ancestor might have lived, the common ancestor of the African ape and hominid lineage. The idea is that you count up the number of mutations that you have seen in the lab date, and then you impose a clocklike rate of mutation, of change over time, to get to the modern point of diversity. So this involves all of that technical sort of process, and then drawing trees of ancestry and imposing a time upon them to account for the modern diversity that we have today, and that's how the 200,000 years was come up with.

However, subsequent genetic testing using mtDNA, also, casts doubt on the precise method that came up with the 200,000-year-old conclusion about mitochondrial Eve. Of course, when the headlines were made about mitochondrial Eve, the first thing that happens is you get competing teams of scientists that rush into their laboratories to try to replicate the process and the outcome, and the replication didn't actually happen. The mitochondrial Eve theory was very popular until about 1992 when three other labs came out with tests that showed something very interesting: specifically, that other trees of ancestry drawn in slightly different ways could account for the same mtDNA diversity in the world today.

In other words, the 200,000-year-old time period was not a firm one, and there was even some question about whether we needed to be pointing to Africa or not. There's a great deal of technical expertise needed to work with these molecules in the lab, far more than I or most biological anthropologists have. It takes a team working with geneticists. Suffice to say that there was a lot of dissent, and the whole mitochondrial Eve field has been thrown into some doubt.

So the question that emerges is, is mitochondrial Eve a valid concept, or is it not? As is usual in the world, there's not a black-and-white answer. There's some yes and some no in part of the answer. First of all, it is misleading, in my view, to imply that there was one specific modern human female who was the mother of us all. Think of what this term, this nickname that the headlines have used, has implied, that there was one, woman progenitor; and she was given a very biblical-sounding name to make it even worse.

I say "worse" because that's very confusing. It gives a misleading picture. Much like the term "missing link" has been misleading in ways that I've described for you before, I think mitochondrial Eve gives us the wrong idea. After all, mitochondrial Eve, whenever she was supposed to have lived, would have had her own ancestors, and remember that there were lots of women living at the same time as she did. Some of them would have gone mitochondrially extinct.

To see why, I'll ask you a question that I often ask my students when I'm teaching this topic, "Do any of you come from families where there are just sons, where the mom and the dad have produced sons but not daughters?" In that case, the mother of the family, though enjoying reproductive success, has no mitochondrial DNA inheritance going. The mitochondria from that woman will be extinct because there are no daughters to pass it along to. So we really need to envision a kind of theme of biological anthropology, an original population rather than an original person.

However, it's interesting to note that even though the other genetic tests have come up with some variable results, they do tend to converge—most of them; not all of them—most of them do tend to converge on Africa between the years of about 400,000 and 100,000 years ago for origins of modern humans. This is true whether you use mtDNA or whether you use the Y-chromosome, which, as you'll remember, is a marker of maleness and is passed along only in the paternal line, so it's a kind of complement on the other side of the equation, if you will.

So the robust finding does, in a broad sense, seem to support the Out-of-Africa replacement model when we look overall at the genetics, although there are still questions and although there are disputes internally about the results. So what we have is a rather chaotic picture when we take the evidence and we look at the two models.

So what do we do? First of all, we keep looking for more evidence from the fossils, the dating of the sites, and the genetics. Another possible solution is to embrace a type of intermediate model. I emphasize that the Out-of-Africa model is quite sharply drawn in contrast to the multiregional model. Might there be something in the middle?

Yes. There's something called the *partial replacement model*, and in this third model, *Homo sapiens* did originate in Africa and did migrate north after having been the initial modern population, but along the way, although there was replacement, it's a very different type of replacement. It's replacement with interbreeding, replacement with hybridization, so that replacement occurred gradually and basically subsumed the genetic material of the other hominids. It integrated or absorbed the other populations rather than simply being a flat-out out-competition or domination.

This is a less extreme model. It does bring elements of both models, and it is probably worth a lot of consideration rather than staking out a claim on one strong side or the other. It will be very interesting to continue the type of DNA analysis that I talked about before, when I talked about Neandertals, to find out which species, which different species in this whole time period might have interbred with each other. That will be very, very important because a lot of these models turn, not only on the dating, but also on the question of whether modern humans would have, in the early stages, interbred with other hominid forms.

Returning then to a familiar refrain for this course, we can sum up our discussion of the two models by saying that we biological anthropologists have produced some good testable predictions. This has over and over again been seen to be important, that the modeling itself is an important part of biological anthropology. What we can do now is go out and work against these specific predictions. We know what to look for. The models set up a framework for us in knowing what to look for.

I want to spend a little bit of time at the end of this lecture summing up, not the lecture per se, but this whole last chunk of the course that has talked in some detail about hominids and hominid evolution, because we're leaving the hominids at the end of this lecture. So recall that we started out at seven million years ago with a new find that's in the country of Chad, the *Sahelanthropus* find that is so new that it's not in any textbook. As far as we can see, this is our best bet for the starting point of the hominid lineage after the split with the common ancestor, and we have gone through all of the intermediate hominids—if you'll call them that—all the different populations.

We know that there are coexisting parallel lineages. We've talked many times about how there's not linear succession but a great deal of evolutionary action going on all over the place; and then we got to 125,000 years ago, and that's the origins of modern *Homo sapiens*. We're leaving our chronology or our timeline right about 30,000 years ago—28,000/30,000. This is the time when we no longer see Neandertals in the fossil record, as I mentioned.

Another way to put that is that this is the time period from which *Homo sapiens* become the only human or humanlike creature on the earth; and of course to us, this is a perfectly natural circumstance. It's somewhat of a change in perspective for us to think any other way. For 30,000 years, we've been used to being *the* humans, or *the* hominid—or however you want to put it—on the earth, but this is extremely recent in evolutionary time. It's an extremely new condition for the human line to have only one species on the earth.

It's really very interesting. I have spent a lot of time thinking about what the world would be like and what life would be like if this weren't the case, if there were some other form—let's just say for the sake of argument, like a Neandertal, somewhat like us but in other ways not—coexisting on the earth with us.

So we leave the hominid chronology at about 30,000 years ago, and what we're going to do now is to talk about a subject in the next lecture that's very dear to my heart, the evolution of language. It is a lecture in which we will bring back reference to some hominids, but we are going to not be talking about the sort of chronological sequence so much. What remains to be seen is to kind of bring together some of the anatomical and behavioral evidence in one lecture to ask about how speech and language might have evolved in the hominid lineage.

Lecture Eighteen
Language

Scope:

We humans can hardly imagine our daily lives without being able to express our ideas verbally (or through signed languages). Language underpins our most human experiences, from watching the performance of a Shakespearean play to exchanging news of our experiences at work, home, or school with loved ones at the end of a day. Language is the keystone of human culture. Biological anthropologists are, thus, keenly interested in finding out whether it is a trait unique to modern humans or has a longer evolutionary history.

The dominant view in linguistics, philosophy, cultural anthropology, and related disciplines tends to be that language is indeed confined entirely to our own species. In this view, production and comprehension of syntax or complex grammatical patterns must be evident before any sort of communication can be defined as language.

Another view posits that language developed gradually within the hominid lineage. Hominid anatomy, hominid behavior, and evolutionary reconstructions may all be marshaled in favor of this gradualist viewpoint. Some biological anthropologists extend this continuity perspective even farther, pointing out that monkey and ape communication includes elements of language.

Inarguably, some aspects of human language are unprecedented in the primate world. Humans have vast vocabularies with which to discuss not only the present, but also the past and future, sometimes using complex narratives. We will explore, using one reasonable (if speculative) model, how such abilities might have evolved.

Outline

I. Language involves far more than just conveying information; we humans experience and even construct our lives through language.

   A. Language is the basis for human sociality. Whether vocal or signed, language shapes our world.

B. Language is such a fundamental part of the human adaptation that we routinely engage in "conversation" with infants, pets, and computers.

C. Children learn immensely complicated languages with little apparent effort. How this process is accomplished is fiercely debated; for our purposes, we should note that even the youngest infants live in a linguistic world.

II. Three distinct possibilities can be envisioned in biological anthropology for how this fundamental human adaptation might have come about. Each is tied to a different understanding of the definition of language.

    A. Language is unique to modern humans and of recent evolutionary origin.

      1. The complex grammatical patterns of syntax are the key element of language; without them, language cannot exist.

      2. Only the modern human brain is capable of generating and comprehending syntactical utterances. Thus, only modern humans can possibly have language.

      3. Significant discontinuity exists between human language and all other forms of hominid, as well as animal, communication.

    B. Language is unique to the hominid lineage but not unique to modern humans; early *Homo* might have had, and certainly Neandertals and later transitional forms did have, language.

      1. Language should not be equated with syntax. We cannot know when syntax evolved, but a broader view of language is more compatible with an evolutionary perspective.

      2. Both anatomical and behavioral clues point to hominids as capable of language. These clues range from the position of various organs in the hominid vocal tract, to details of hominid brain anatomy, to known hominid behaviors that would have required some linguistic capability to perform.

      3. Significant continuity exists across hominids, and between early and later forms of *Homo*, but significant discontinuity exists between hominid language and all other forms of animal communication.

C. Language, or significant elements of language, can be found in primates even before the evolutionary split between hominids and great apes.

   1. An evolutionary perspective compels us to understand that language emerged gradually, with no major Rubicon crossed at the starting point of the hominid lineage. We may view language either as composed of various critical components or as complex communication that results in cohesive social groupings.

   2. Either of these definitions of language allows us to find language in monkeys and apes today. Some wild monkey populations, together with the enculturated apes, offer the best illustrations.

   3. Complex nonhuman primate communication is related to human language by homology; the relationship between the two is unlike that between communication of primates and of all other animals, even, for instance, dolphins.

III. The human species-specific form of language is without a doubt different, even if only by degree and not by kind, from all other communication systems. Viable step-by-step evolutionary scenarios exist for a gradual development of this human adaptation.

   A. Only human language relies on large vocabularies comprised of words with specific, widely understood meanings. These words are used in ways that not only convey information in the present, but reflect on the past and plan for the future.

   B. The emergence of these special abilities need not be thought of as mysterious or wholly disconnected from evolutionarily prior systems of communication. A scenario proposed by the anthropologist Robbins Burling includes key steps that might explain the necessary evolutionary shifts.

   1. The evolutionary base is provided by the iconic gesturing of great apes (see Lecture Seven).

   2. With increased brain size and an increased ability over that of the great apes to imitate actions of others, hominids would have been better able to adopt utterances made by social companions and use them in a socially conventional way. The need for reliance on iconic signs would have decreased.

3. Over time, linguistic signs would become more and more arbitrary—breaking the link between a sign and its referent. Words could begin to refer to specific objects, events, or actions.
4. Eventually, using words in orderly combinations would have become more and more beneficial, leading to the development of syntax.
5. Burling clearly admits this scenario is speculative, but it does dovetail nicely with data from primate studies, as well as with evolutionary logic.
6. As with all other hypothetical scenarios that we have reviewed, this one both requires more data and stimulates more research. The creation of plausible scenarios is an important part of the ongoing work in biological anthropology today.

Essential Reading:

King, *The Origins of Language,* especially chapter by Burling (second half) and King's chapter 2.

Questions to Consider:

1. Which of the three views of language do you find most convincing? Why?
2. What specific type of hominid discovery do you think would most help clarify the origins of language?

Lecture Eighteen—Transcript
Language

Finally, language. We've talked about everything in the hominid lineage, from technology to art to bipedalism, but we have not talked about the evolution of language, and we will do so now. I have preferred to give language its own separate lecture in accordance with its significance, and to place it in the course at this point, after we have gone through the basics of hominid chronology.

I do this because language is so critically important to modern humans. Language involves far more than just the conveying of information or the sending of messages. I believe, as do most scholars, that language is the way that we construct our lives and experience our lives, and I say this whether we're talking about Shakespearean language, elegant plays and poetry, or merely talking about our dinner table conversation at the end of the day. It's important to all of us. It's how we come to know others and, I would say, come to know ourselves as well. In other words, language is the basis for human sociality.

I try to remember to use the term language instead of speech. I don't always catch myself, but I want to, because I want to include both vocal and signed language. People can use both or either, and in either case, it doesn't matter. Language shapes our world and connects us to others.

Language is such a fundamental part of the human adaptation that we find ourselves sometimes addressing other beings or other objects that have no hope of comprehending or responding. I'm thinking here about talking to babies, to pets, even to machines. Let's face it. We do talk to the littlest tiny babies who cannot comprehend our words, who can't respond. Yes, they might be able to follow along with a voice tone or a facial expression, but they can't understand the words that we use.

You could say, "But an infant is going to grow up, and you're teaching it, basically, by talking to it." What about a pet? Again, the argument could be made that pets will understand voice tone; but using myself as an example, I will submit that many people will talk to animals in full, complex sentences with words and meaning.

For example, in my life, I have uttered sentences such as, "Now rabbit, you cannot keep chewing through the modem cords of my computer, so please stop." There's not much about voice tone here that we're trying to get across. I live with, in addition to a husband and daughter, three cats and a rabbit; and I do find myself talking to all of those creatures, knowing that they cannot respond in the same way that I'm talking to them, and that they understand only some parts of what I'm saying.

You might ask yourself—those of you who are computer users—have you ever talked, in a fit of rage or otherwise, to your computers? I think the point I'm making is obvious about the depth of our adaptation through language; that it's just what we do, no matter to whom we are speaking.

Another corollary of this involves the topic of children. Children learn our immensely complicated languages all around the world with little direct instruction. It appears to be relatively effortless for young infants to do this, and we don't sit them down to teach them this. How this process of language acquisition is accomplished is fiercely debated. It would be the subject of an entire course on its own.

What we want to know is what I've already said, that the youngest infants, even from birth, already live in a linguistic world. I don't believe that we should make a distinction between pre-linguistic and linguistic when it comes to children. "Pre-linguistic" is sometimes used for the youngest children that don't yet have speech. They may babble or have facial expressions or turn-taking in a sort of pre-speech type of way, but that transition, while important for language theorists, for us, we should see it all as just part of growing up in a language-filled world.

The human brain, even from infancy as I have said before, is adapted to absorb information. We are adapted to enter into relationship with our social partners, and it is through language that we do that. So a key question for biological anthropology is, at what point do we see evidence for language in the hominid lineage?

Three distinct possibilities can be envisioned to understand how language might have come about. They key thing to know is that each possibility is tied to a quite different definition of language. I want to go through the three possibilities with you, and tie each one to a slightly different understanding of what language is all about.

On the first view, language is unique to modern humans. It is a *Homo sapiens* phenomenon that evolved only with our species, and therefore it is of recent evolutionary origin. Typically, the definition of language that goes along with this view is that language should be equated with syntax, so that without syntax, language does not exist. The complex grammatical patterns of syntax are the key here.

Syntax is often defined or loosely understood as word order, the order of the words that come in a sentence, but in fact, the definition that we need to use is a little bit more complicated, because the full definition of syntax should involve the relationship of elements in a sentence; for example, how the clauses relate to the main part of a sentence, what kind of hierarchical relationship there is among the elements of a sentence, what modifies what.

Let's take a fairly complex sentence. I'll make one up: "The ape with the hurt leg that just made a gesture is the alpha male of the community." I think most people can follow that sentence. It's a little bit tangled, but from a syntactical point of view, it's complicated. The syntax—there are all those clauses, the parts that are embedded within other parts of the sentence, and that's what syntax is all about.

On this first view of language being unique to modern humans, only the modern human brain is capable of generating and dealing with syntax. So by definition, only modern humans can have language. On this view, syntax is governed by a system of rules that are literally ingrained in the human brain. It's something that's hardwired in there. It's an instinct, if you will, to be able to see the world, deal with the world and interact with the world syntactically. So it's just as much a part of our brains as is our neocortex, the particular part of the brain most involved with thinking and cognition.

So the conclusion can only be, from this first possibility, one of discontinuity, that modern humans are set apart from everything else in the world, including other hominids, certainly including non-human primates and any other type of animal. So there's a gap between modern humans and absolutely everybody else.

What follows from this is it doesn't make sense to talk about gradual, incremental evolution of language. You either have it—hardwired rules for syntax in the brain—or you don't. It's similarly not sensible to talk about language as we know it, as if there could be some precursor type of form. This first view is very hard and fast on what language is. It's pretty cut-and-dry.

For the most part, this first view tends to be problematic for biological anthropologists. We know better than to make full generalizations like that, but on the average, I would say that most biological anthropologists worry about such a hard and fast view because it does not engage with evolutionary questions. It doesn't even believe that there is a search that is reasonable to undertake for precursors, if we are already tying language to a human brain, specifically.

So let's go on with the second of our three possibilities. This is one that is more compatible with a certain type of evolutionary thinking. So number two: language is now seen as being unique to the hominid lineage, but not necessarily just to *Homo sapiens*, so that earlier hominids probably did have language, and we can trace that in various ways in the fossils or the behaviors. Possibility number two says, let's break away from this litmus test definition of language as being equivalent to syntax. We shouldn't make that narrow equation. A broader view of what language is all about is more compatible with evolutionary theory.

Here, typically the search is for the origins of speech, and I do use this word quite purposefully. In other words, it's much easier to look for vocal tract or brain configurations for speech, most people think, than it would be to look for some sort of gestural or signed language. This isn't to say that there are not theorists who talk about the origins of gesture and non-vocal communication, but rather that the typical search in fossil hominids has been for something that we can tie to capabilities for speech.

So we're going to review a sampling of both anatomical and behavioral clues to whether hominids, and which hominids, might have been capable of language. These clues do range from vocal tract to brain to behavior. We'll start with the vocal tract. The vocal tract is a soft tissue area of the body, primarily composed of three important structures: the tongue, the larynx and the pharynx. The tongue is obvious. We know that the larynx is the voice box, and just to remind you of basic biology, the pharynx is the combined opening to the stomach and the lungs.

In almost all mammals—including cats, dogs, monkeys, apes, those kinds of things—we see that the larynx is located fairly high up in the neck or high up in the throat, and it has a particular relationship to the pharynx and the tongue. That means that there are few sounds that are capable of being made. In other words, there are sounds that come out, but they're not articulated speech sounds because the larynx is high up and it does not articulate with the pharynx and the tongue in the way that is required for sharp, discreet speech sounds to be made.

Biological anthropologists have analyzed the skulls of hominids and found that up until right about *Homo erectus*, that very same vocal tract plan was in place, so let's say for australopithecines and *Homo habilis*, a mammalian-like, cat-like, monkey-like, ape-like vocal tract without the ability for sharply discriminated speech sounds.

You might ask, "There's a problem here, isn't there? You're looking at skulls, but you're trying to trace the origins of something that's soft tissue. How does that work?" As it turns out, of course we don't have *Homo erectus* larynxes and pharynxes. We don't find those, but there are clues in the bony structures of the skull to the position of the larynx, so if you're a real anatomical whiz, you can turn a skull over, look at the skull base, and look at small, bony projections that will indicate where the larynx would have resided, so to speak, in the vocal tract.

So there tends to be the view here that, starting with *Homo erectus*, there was a so-called "descent of the larynx" towards its modern human position. We have a larynx located much lower down in the throat or the neck, so that it articulates differently with the pharynx and the tongue to produce the speech sounds that we know. It's interesting to note that when modern human babies are born, their larynx is actually quite high, and it descends during development in life, and this is part of the reason why they become better at articulation in their first months of life. But in any case, we have an indicator here through fossil evidence that there could have been yet another shift point at *Homo erectus*.

However, there are some contentious facts about *Homo erectus* that should be entered into the record here, and we need to return for a moment to the Nariokotome Boy, the fossil dated to 1.6 million years ago found in Kenya that's so complete, 80 percent complete. One thing that researchers have focused on is the fact that this individual had a relatively small opening through the vertebrae in the back, through which the spinal cord would have passed. This led them to interpret, to look at that evidence and come up with a suggestion that the spinal cord itself would have been fairly small or thin, and from there they go on to speculate that there would have been less control by the spinal cord of the so-called intercostal muscles. These are muscles around the ribs that control breathing.

If, in fact, the spinal cord was relatively weak in its control of these muscles for breathing, the view is that speech might have been compromised, that there might have not been a lot of power, muscularly, to produce speech. So the vocal tract evidence suggests a shift, but this other evidence of spinal cord and muscles leaves us with a type of question. Remember that the Nariokotome Boy is the single-most complete *Homo erectus*. We don't have a lot of other fossil evidence to compare that with.

There are other ways to analyze fossils, as well. I'll give you just one more quick example. If you flip over a skull and you look at the skull base, there's a small opening that is called the hypoglossal canal, and it is through this small opening that the nerves run to the tongue, so they enervate or enliven the tongue; and if you measure the size of this opening, biological anthropologists have determined that the origins of speech are most likely not with *Homo erectus*, but only later with Neandertal. In other words, the size of the opening gives us an understanding of how enervated, how nerve-rich, the tongue would have been. So as with most everything else in anthropology, we come up with slightly different answers, depending on the source of data.

Yet, I would say that there is still a type of convergence. We have an enormous time period of hominid evolution, and the convergence for origins of speech tends to be on *Homo erectus* and Neandertal, not on the earlier hominids, and that is interesting and important in its own right. So on this second possibility that we have spent some time talking about, significant continuity exists across at least some of the hominids in this later time period.

We might also want to mention here that some of the behavior that *Homo erectus* and Neandertal engaged in—we can easily speculate—shores up this idea that they might have had some type of speech. Once we're talking about things like deliberate burial or long distance migration; it's easy to convince ourselves that maybe they would have needed speech. This is a speculative thinking, but it all tends to fit together.

This leaves us with possibility number three, and here there is an even greater extension of capabilities of language to other organisms. Here, language, or at least significant elements of it, can be found in primates. It's very important to please keep in mind during this section as I talk about this that I'll be talking about present-day monkeys and apes but I'm using them as stand-ins, as reference for creatures who would have lived before the evolutionary split between the African apes and the hominid lineage. We can only look at language capabilities in the modern animals that we have now.

On this view, an evolutionary perspective compels us to understand that there was no major watershed, that language would have evolved quite gradually, even starting back before the hominids. So we can view language in two different ways. It's really fair of me to explain that there are two kinds of sub-definitions of language within this area. In the first, language is composed of a series of traits or features. We might look at, for example, environmental reference, the idea that you can make reference to certain things in the environment, or we might look for some type of syntax in language, even. We might look for learnability of language or modifiability of language, and then we go out and we search for those things in monkey and ape communication.

A slightly different view, which happens to fall more in line with my own research, is that language is not just a collection of traits but that it's most important in use and that language is about dynamic change and cohesion. In other words, language is important for what it accomplishes, and what it accomplishes is coordination of social action between partners, dynamically.

No matter which slightly different view of language you choose, here we go out and we look for what monkeys and apes do, and we find examples that fit both sub-definitions. You might remember that we talked earlier about the fact that some monkeys, when they're interacting, scream in ways that encode information about the environment, about their social partners, or possibly about predators or about food sources. My own work with gestures in great apes, as I've discussed, shows that gestures can be used as well as vocalizations to coordinate at quite a complex and subtle level what's going on between social partners in the great apes. So either of these definitions allows us to find language or its precursors in monkey and ape populations.

Complex non-human primate communication can be related to human language, on this view, by homology. In other words, we're really talking about systems that arose through shared descent. The fact is that we arise from common stock with these creatures. So the claim on this third view is that we evolved language from a very important evolutionary starting base, just as we evolved other things based on the primate grasping hand or the primate depth perception, the primate brain, that we have talked about. So homology is a key corollary of the third view.

Whichever one of these three possibilities seems more sensible to you, we want to conclude this section of the lecture by emphasizing one point. None of these three views wants to deny human uniqueness. None of them says that there's something about language that's so continuous with other primates that it doesn't set apart humans, so we want to be able to both at the same time account evolutionarily for the language that we use, but to recognize that it is not exactly like precursor forms.

For example, as far as we know, only humans rely on large vocabularies that have specific and distinct meanings, and these words are used in very complicated, intricate ways, with long narratives and storytelling possible. My favorite candidate for a feature of language—or an aspect of language use, more precisely— is that only humans have the ability to talk about the past and the future. We can enter into conversation with others and share memories. If two people have a long history together, they can sit back and reflect about things that they shared, or one person meeting a new friend might want to talk about his past and bring that other person into his internal reflective world through talking about his own memories.

Similarly, there's strategic planning that can go on for the future. This is very much part of human nature, to talk and plan and think about what is coming ahead. We don't think that there's a good deal of evidence showing that hominids or great apes could do this. It would be hard to know, in some cases. It's easier to make that statement for great apes than it is for hominids, but there seems to be something that was quite elaborated late in the human evolutionary line.

However, what I want to do is talk about a scenario of evolution of language that can still derive these unique features from a continuous base of evolution. Remember that we're working with this tricky balance—unique features—but we don't want to make them mysterious or enigmatic, or as if they could not have been derived evolutionarily.

You'll notice that what I'm doing here is I'm clearly siding against possibility number one, in which language is syntax and is uniquely modern and only in the human brain, so I am speaking from my position a someone who writes a lot about evolution of language—my bias, if you will—that there is some type of continuity in language evolution. So when I give you a plausible scenario for language origins, as I'm about to do, I don't just pick one at random. I pick one that I like. I pick my favorite one, and it's going to reflect some continuity.

The scenario for language origins in evolution that I will describe for you was created by the anthropologist Robbins Burling, and he explains in a very detailed way key steps that can get us to human language through a series of evolutionary shifts. I invited Robbins Burling, along with eight other people and myself, to an evolution of language seminar that was held in 1996. This was held at a wonderful institute in Santa Fe, New Mexico called the School of American Research.

I had written my dissertation there and was later funded by the school to bring together 10 scholars from various disciplines, various states and various countries, to come together for five days to talk about origins and evolution of language. I have to tell you that there's nothing better for academics than to be flown to a beautiful city, put up and stored and housed on a beautiful campus with good food, with five full days of no distractions and nothing to do than to talk about something that is important to you: in this case, evolution of language.

Robbins Burling came, participated and contributed to the book that resulted from this seminar. Here's what he had to say. Burling starts us out in this quest to really delineate the steps and origins of language with apes. He starts out at a starting point that we have mentioned before as well, and that is the iconic gesturing of apes. Burling uses a slightly different term for iconic gesturing. He refers to it as *motivated signing*, but we are going to use them as equivalent terms. Iconic gesturing and motivated signing are the same thing.

You'll remember that iconic gestures are ones that in some way depict the action that is being made or requested. So an iconic gesture might be something like putting the arm forward and making a "come here" gesture, or by making a rotational "turn around" type of gesture in the air. The gesture depicts the action, so it's pictorial in a certain sense. Great apes can do iconic gestures, we know, and Burling calls this a very key ability that sets apart the great apes from other primates such as monkeys, and from other animals as well.

There's a shift at the start of the hominid lineage that Burling finds important, and this shift relates to both increased brain size—so I am talking about *Homo habilis* here, not earlier australopithecines—*Homo habilis* increased brain size and increased imitative capability. Oddly enough, we have found out somewhat to our surprise, that apes are not particularly good at aping, at imitating. Some are. I wouldn't say that it's a completely absent type of skill; but for the most part, apes do not do particularly well imitating skills or gestures or vocalizations of others.

So Burling envisions, as many other anthropologists do, a leap in this capability at some point in relatively early human evolution; and the key to this is the fact that it would have resulted in a reduced reliance on iconic signs. If you can imitate, then you can collectively work towards a conventional system where not everything has to be depicted in space, but there can just be symbolic type of collective understanding, so that there would be an increased ability to adopt utterances, whether vocal or gestural, made by social companions.

Over time, these signs, as we now will call them, these linguistic utterances, would become more and more arbitrary; in other words, not pictorial but arbitrary, without a necessary relationship between what is uttered and the actual object or event referred to. Words could emerge, or gestures, that could begin to refer to very specific objects, events or actions, and again, the key is to remember we're talking about social conventionalization, these hominid brains' paying attention to other hominids, absorbing what others are doing, imitating, coming to a collective understanding. Eventually, vocabularies would have built up, and using words in orderly combinations would have become more and more beneficial.

Again, we want to insert the concept of reproductive success here, that it is possible that those hominids that were able to speak and use words in this way could have improved, for example, their ability to find mates, their ability to talk about survival against predators or survival in hunting, in such a way that it could have resulted in a reproductive advantage. So you get syntax at the end of this scenario emerging from all of the evolutionary steps that went before, but it is not mysterious. It does not have to be hardwired suddenly in the human brain, but rather, it comes out of all the steps that were prior.

Of course, Burling admits that this is in some ways speculative; however, parts are quite testable. The parts that I have described for you fit very nicely with both the non-human primate data and with evolutionary logic. As with all the other hypothetical scenarios we've been reviewing in this course—and there have been quite a few—this one at the same time both requires more data and will stimulate more research, and that's exactly what we would require a good evolutionary scenario to do.

I think there is a role for scenarios like this, as I have said so many times. So I will conclude by reaffirming my particular conclusion that there has been significant continuity over evolutionary time in the development of language, and this is again one of those times when we really see the articulation of different sub-areas of biological anthropology: the primatology, the paleoanthropological literature and evidence, and so forth.

We are going to make a big transition in this course, because the last chunk of lectures will turn to a very different focus. We are going to move a little bit away from the very direct consideration of our evolutionary past and move to the present, but our focus will be asking how the present has been affected by our evolutionary past. We will talk about race, human variation, evolution of human diet and so forth. We'll begin with race in the next lecture.

Lecture Nineteen
Do Human Races Exist?

Scope:

In the final lectures, we shift gears again to consider ways in which biological anthropology explicitly interacts with issues in today's modern world. We start with a question that may be a surprising one: Do human races exist?

Contemporary biological anthropologists have achieved a near-consensus in answering this question: No matter how sociologically useful the concept of race may be, there is no biological validity to the idea that human races exist. Whichever way one tries to carve up the human species into discrete races—based on skin color and other genetic attributes—it turns out that there is too much variability *within* each race for the idea to have any biological meaning. The human species is too recent in origin, and too characterized by gene flow and mating between groups, for meaningful biological differences to evolve.

Yet a few prominent scholars refuse to accept the view that race is a biologically invalid concept. They ask us to open our eyes. Races, they say, are immediately distinguishable by the person on the street; why, then, can't biological anthropologists accept reality? Don't race-specific anatomies, behaviors, and diseases exist? Confronting this type of query head on, we will work to understand why it is based on scientifically inadequate thinking about race.

Outline

I. The final section of the course explores topics in biological anthropology that relate to contemporary human populations. We begin with a vexing one: Can the human species be understood as made up of biologically distinct races?

   A. The term *race* is so ingrained in American society that the very question we are asking may take people aback.

   1. As the biological anthropologist Michael Blakey has said, the idea that people can be grouped into races may seem as obvious to us as the sun rising in the east every morning.

2. Since at least the time of Linnaeus, the 18th century Swedish biologist, we have been presented with taxonomies of the human races, and the concept has become second nature.

3. Yet we know that science pushes us to investigate phenomena that are seemingly obvious and to insist on questioning their validity. (After all, the sun doesn't really rise in the sky; this was Blakey's point.)

B. We wish to explore race only from the perspective of biological anthropology.

1. Biologically speaking, a race would represent a group of people sharing genetically determined traits, such as skin color, hair color, eye shape, and nose shape, among others.

2. A race, then, would be an intermediate-level grouping of humans, in between that of the population and that of the species.

3. The sociological and historical validity of race, unlike the biological validity, are not at issue here.

II. Most biological anthropologists today reject the idea that the concept of human race has any biological validity. Race is a socially constructed concept.

A. No agreement exists on how many races can be identified in the world. The possibilities range from 3 to more than 200, based on which traits one deems significant.

B. No such entity as a pure human race exists in the world today; the world's populations constantly intermarry and interbreed.

C. Further, to the best of anthropological knowledge, no such entity as a pure human race ever existed. Gene flow, migration, and interbreeding across populations are all processes with very long histories in the development of our species.

D. Today, more variation exists within so-called races than between them. The best estimate suggests that only 15% of all human genetic variation can be traced to differences between races.

E. History shows us that race is used in socially constructed ways that are divorced from biological reality. The definition of what kind of person "counts" as a member of a certain race changes with historical context.

III. A few scientists today insist that the majority view is wrong. These scientists can be grouped into two camps, one from biological anthropology generally and another from forensic anthropology. They say that racial differences are both obvious and real.

A. According to a few biological anthropologists, obvious evidence exists for the fact of human races.

    1. Compare a man native to Stockholm, Sweden, with one from Dar es Salaam, Tanzania. The obvious differences one sees reflect human biology and race.

    2. *Cluster diseases*, such as sickle cell anemia, much more prevalent in some races than others, cannot be ignored.

    3. Occasionally, these notions extend to claims that different levels of intelligence can be found among different human races.

B. The problem with these views is not that they are politically incorrect. Rather, they reflect poor (and outdated) evolutionary thinking.

    1. The "Stockholm versus Dar es Salaam" test is flawed, in part because it ignores the gradual shifts in populations between these two geographic extremes.

    2. When measuring such factors as disease or intelligence between groups, we must not forget that the groups are not now, and have never been, distinct from each other in the first place. So-called biological differences diminish or disappear when this fact is realized and when overlap between groups is recognized.

C. In the area of applied biological anthropology, forensic anthropologists routinely classify individuals (from their skeletal remains) using the variable of race.

    1. Forensic anthropologists, in analyzing bones, attempt to discern not only an individual's sex and age but also his or her race.

    2. These scientists insist that using such categories as Caucasian-American, African-American, Asian-American, Hispanic, and native American is reliable and beneficial.

3. Most biological anthropologists reply that such classification has limited use. Providing information about race may help in legal matters but tells us little that is valid or genuinely interesting about the individual in question.

D. The New York African Burial Ground Project shows how biological anthropologists can work with skeletal remains to go well beyond a focus on racial traits.

1. Project scientists have analyzed more than 400 skeletons from enslaved individuals who died and were buried in Manhattan during the 17th and 18th centuries.

2. The project's focus has been to explore the culture and history of an important human population.

IV. Human variation is a fascinating topic, one deserving of study by biological anthropologists. Trying to approach it by way of racial variation is inaccurate, but other avenues are available, and we turn to these in the next lecture.

Essential Reading:

Jurmain et al., *Introduction to Physical Anthropology*, chapter 15, pp. 410–20 and 437–38.

Marks, *What It Means to Be 98% Chimpanzee*, chapters 4–7.

Supplementary Reading:

Blakey, "Bioarchaeology of the African Diaspora in the Americas."

Questions to Consider:

1. Of what significance to the discussion of race is the long human history of gene flow, migration, and intergroup mating?

2. From the perspective of biological anthropology, what is wrong with a statement such as "Asian-Americans are more intelligent than European-Americans?"

Lecture Nineteen—Transcript
Do Human Races Exist?

Starting with Lecture Nineteen, we head in a slightly different direction in order to engage with other topics in biological anthropology. In this final section of the course we will explore issues that relate to contemporary human populations. It's probably worth noting at this point why the course leaves off at about 30,000 years ago in terms of the hominids that we have been talking about. We just finished up talking about hominid language, and we stopped with the whole hominid spectrum at 30,000 years ago, with modern *Homo sapiens* dominating the world in terms of the human-type lineages.

This is one of those disciplinary boundary issues. In other words, biological anthropology leaves it up to other parts of anthropology and to history to talk about what happened after 30,000 years ago. The invention of agriculture, the initiation of domestic animals, all of these things are important topics in prehistory, but they don't tend to be studied by biological anthropologists. They're studied by archaeologists and also by historians who are interested in the origins of writing and that sort of thing. So this is an explanation for why we are shifting direction at this point.

The first topic we'll consider in this final section of the course has to do with race. The question before us is, can the human world, the human populations on earth, be carved up into biologically distinct races? For some people, this is a somewhat odd question. Some people would ask, "Isn't it obvious? Look around the world. Isn't it clear that people of different races exist in the world?" After all, the term race is completely ingrained in the American vocabulary. It's just part of our lives. We want to consider this very question in Lecture Nineteen.

As the biological anthropologist Michael Blakey has said, that people can be grouped into races may seem as obvious to us as the fact that the sun rises in the east every morning. Part of the reason for this is that the idea of taxonomic categorization of races has been with us for so very long. It's been with us for centuries, scientifically. We know that the 18th century Swedish anatomist Linnaeus was the first to come up with a very scientifically based categorization of people according to race.

Before this time period, others had used racial categorizations based on, for example, skin color. If we look at the ancient Egyptians, we find that they referred to themselves as red people and talked about other societies surrounding them in the world as white and black and yellow. But with Linnaeus in the 1700s, we get a very specific scheme. You'll recall he's the very person who gave us the binomial system for calling ourselves *Homo sapiens*, for calling Lucy *Australopithecus afarensis*, and so on.

He went much further than that with his typology of human races. He suggested that there are four major human races that can be divided up according to geography and skin color. He called *Homo europaeus* the first race—not in terms of chronology; this is just a list of his races—these were white people of Europe. *Homo afer*, the black race of Africa; *Homo asiaticus*, yellow people of Asia, and *Homo americanus*, red people of America. Very simple: skin color times geography, and that was the answer for him.

Yet, even though we're so used to thinking about race, and we have had various taxonomies that have grown out of the one that Linnaeus had done. In other words, people have played around with that particular classification; we know that science pushes us to ask questions, even when things seem obvious. To continue with the words that Michael Blakey uses, after all, we know that the sun doesn't really rise every morning, does it? Every schoolchild knows that it may seem as if we get the sun rising and crossing the sky, but that is not really what's happening, scientifically. Similarly, we need to look harder at the phenomenon of race.

We wish to explore race only from a biological anthropology perspective; and biologically speaking, a race would represent a grouping of people in between the species level and the population level. It would be some kind of cluster that would be an intermediate level between those two. So by this definition then, a race would be a cluster of people with some genetically determined traits that they have in common: skin color, hair color, possibly even body shape, nose shape, eye shape. Any number of these things would be held in common by a group of people living in a particular area or being able to trace their origins back to that particular area.

We want to emphasize that when we talk about race, limiting ourselves to biological anthropology in assessing the concept is important to keep in mind. Sociologically and historically, there's no question that the concept of race is useful. It would be very difficult to talk about American history without recourse to the concept of race, but we are going to confine ourselves only to the question of biological validity.

Finally, at this point in the course, I can tell you that there is a topic on which almost all biological anthropologists agree—a rare situation—and it is not 100 percent consensus, as we will hear, but it is relatively close. Most biological anthropologists today reject the idea that the concept of human race has any biological validity. Instead, they maintain that race is a purely socially constructed concept, and must be kept in the realm of sociology, history and so on.

Why? I want to present a series of arguments that support the rejection of race as valid biologically. What evidence do biological anthropologists marshal to support what they say? First, there's no agreement at all as to how many races we should be identifying in the world. We started out noting that Linnaeus some time ago came up with four, but you could compile a whole textbook just on the basis of the different types of taxonomies that have been delineated. Some have only three races. There have been others that have over 200 races. This is obviously a subjective thing. One decides what's important, and then clumps people on the basis of subjective decisions.

For example, let's consider the Indian subcontinent. There are people in India who have skin color darker than some people living in Africa. They also have facial features that appear to be somewhat Caucasoid-like—Caucasian-like, white-like, if you will—but they live in Asia. What would Linnaeus have done with these people? You've got them in one place, but their skin color looks like they should be someplace else, and their facial features would point to yet a third place. This is a simple example, but we can see that there are all kinds of disagreement about simply how to do the carving or where to draw the lines.

Second, we know to a certainty that there's no such thing as a pure human race in the world today. There is too much intermarriage, interbreeding and gene flow among the various groups that exist; and the idea that there is some race somewhere in the forest, mythically primitive, that's been held apart from all of society or was any time recently, is just that. It's mythical. Even more, there has been no known entity as a pure human race any time in human prehistory, and this may be more surprising. This is a claim I'm making calibrated to our best anthropological knowledge.

The idea here is that there's a very long history of gene flow, migration and interbreeding, so that our human history is one of mixing from the very start of our species; and remember, that that's not really such a long time ago, 125,000 years ago to begin with. Both the multiregional and the partial replacement models that I talked about last time for the origins of *Homo sapiens* depend deeply on hybridization or interbreeding. That is the way those models are conceiving of our origins. Whether that is true or not is still an open question, but we do know from the time of *Homo sapiens*, early on, that there's been a lot of migration, movement and intermarriage.

We can also think back to times in our more recent past that have been studied by historians as well as anthropologists. You might think of a phenomenon such as the Silk Road, this very famous trade route that started in China and went across 7000 miles of space, of land, to end at the Mediterranean. The Silk Road was highly active as a trade route starting in about the second century B.C., and there were movements of peoples all along this road, back and forth over vast differences in space, and not only the objects then moved, but also the people and their genes, and interbreeding and all sorts of things happened.

These are just some examples to back up the claim that we shouldn't think that there were human races that were pure and isolated at some point before, but that that has somehow disappeared. The better idea is just to think of migration and interbreeding all along.

Another central fact: it has been found in quite a robust and convincing manner, that if you look at variation in the world today, only about 15 percent of human genetic variation occurs between races. Fully 85 percent of such genetic variation occurs within a race. To be honest, it took me a while to really believe this. I had to read it a whole lot.

But consider this. Two people may be grouped into the same race based simply on skin color. This seems to be a particular feature that Americans, especially, are very keyed into. So you may say, "Look at two people who have the same skin color. They should be in the same race," whereas, in fact, in our example, the two people share almost nothing else: no other genetic origins, no geographic place of origin. They may have completely different traits otherwise; and in fact, their genetic variability is quite great, even though superficially, the skin color is the same. So the cultural history may vary, and the genetics may vary, very much within a race.

History tells us something as well about the way that the term *race* has been used. We mentioned before that biological anthropologists say that race is socially constructed. The arguments I've just given you are meant to attempt to be convincing that race is not biologically valid, but we also must recognize a fact that is crystal clear historically. The definition of what kind of person counts as being part of a race changes with historical context, and it is not only subjective, but has been used with quite conscious manipulation of power.

The history of biological anthropology is, if you go back far enough—I'm not talking about recent decades—unfortunately also the history of racism. Race, for a long time, by biological anthropologists and other scientists, was used to construct the "other," if you will. Race was used to divide the single human species, to set some people apart as better, and some as worse; some as superior, some as inferior.

Let's go back to the example of Linnaeus for a moment, with his four races divided by skin color and geography. In fact, he did go a little bit further as he developed this taxonomy, and he imputed to certain races better qualities. Perhaps unsurprisingly for his time, *Homo europaeus*, the European race, he found to be of superior intellect compared to all others, and this is a theme that we find over and over again.

It's not just the idea that people look different or have different genetic origins, but race has been used to enslave and to dominate, to suggest who should have power, who is lazy, who is smart, who is not, who should govern and who should be governed. So we should have a skepticism and at least a desire to question the use of the concept once we see how it's been used and once we understand the biological facts behind human variation.

I have to admit, as I indicated earlier, that not all biological anthropologists are of this view, and it's only fair to include the minority viewpoint here. A few scientists disagree with everything that I have just told you, and these scientists can be divided into two different camps. One is biological anthropologists who are academics or lab scientists who say that race is valid. The other group are forensic anthropologists who are out working practically in the field, using race as a concept, and we want to go through these counter-arguments.

According to some biological anthropologists then, there is obvious evidence for human race. We're back to that point again of evidence being irrefutably obvious, visibly obvious. They would say, "Let's do a simple test. Let's compare a man from Stockholm, Sweden to one living in Dar es Salaam, Tanzania. Let's ignore all the cultural trappings, such as clothing or other contextual factors such as objects." There are obvious differences that are going to be visible that will be markers of race, according to these people. In other words, the skin color, the facial features, the hair, everything else is going to be racial, and that we cannot get away from, in this minority view.

A second point these people suggest is that there are diseases that cluster according to certain races. We have talked before in this course about sickle-cell anemia, and it is true that in this country, the overwhelming majority of the victims of sickle-cell anemia are African-American, so some biological anthropologists say this too, is evidence that race is real.

Occasionally, although not often, there are claims still made that there are racial differences that are measurable and quantifiable, even in intelligence. These are rarely biological anthropologists, but sometimes, and there's a recent series of publications—not by biological anthropologists but by a scientist—insisting that there are measurable differences in IQ and intellect showing that Asians are the smartest race, and Europeans are in the middle, and Africans are at the bottom. This continues to be showing up in publications, although atypically.

What is the problem with this type of view? To start with, some might say they're politically incorrect. Yes, but they may be; they may not be. Who knows? Science does not care about what is politically correct or politically incorrect. We want to evaluate the truth of these statements. If, in fact, there were scientific evidence for them, however uncomfortable they might make us, we would have to investigate them.

However, there are flawed assumptions at the heart of these claims by these minority biological anthropologists—minority in terms of how they think about race. First of all, let's revisit the Stockholm versus Dar es Salaam test. The problem with it is it's picking extremes, and it ignores all the gradual shifts in the middle.

It also completely forgets the fact that you're looking at just these really obvious markers without taking into account all the ways in which two people in Stockholm will be different from each other and two people in Dar es Salaam will be different from each other. There are tremendous ways in which those two individuals in the same place, possibly looking superficially alike, will vary genetically, and that gets lost.

We also must not forget the lesson of the question of pure race. In other words, there never has been a group of people who've been isolated in Stockholm or isolated in Dar es Salaam, and who have not interacted with others. These so-called biological differences that are supposed to be present may not completely disappear, but they diminish in significance when we understand this fact of long mixing between populations and overlap genetically between population or the so-called races.

What about the forensic anthropologists? Here we have the second group of counter-thinkers, people who say, "Yes, I really want to embrace race because I don't want to go with the flow and reject it. I don't believe that that is correct." Forensic anthropologists routinely classify individuals using their skeletal remains in various ways. They want to find out the sex of an individual, age, and also use race quite routinely. You may remember from the introductory lecture that I talked about a forensic anthropologist called Clyde Snow, who does what he calls osteobiography. He reads the bones, whether that's in Argentina or Oklahoma City, all those examples that I gave you of his career.

Forensic anthropologists attempt to discern race because they are trying to solve a question about a person's identity. Forensic anthropologists are often working in a practical arena. They're trying to solve crimes or intersect with the legal system; and in the courts and in police files, race is a very routine category. It's one of those things that just gets used all the time. These scientists, the forensic ones, say that using categories really makes a practical difference, categories such as Caucasian-American, Hispanic, African-

American, or something like this. Native American would be another example. As I understand it, 80 percent of the time, forensic anthropologists can get race correct. They can be accurate about identifying a particular individual to the so-called racial category.

By the way, there's a big interest in American popular culture right now in forensic anthropology. If any of you watch "CSI" on television, as I do, or you may read the books about fictional forensic anthropologists, these techniques are a lot of fun to read about. There's an anthropologist called Kathy Reichs who is a working academic anthropologist who writes very good fiction, a whole series of books about a woman forensic anthropologist who goes out and makes these kinds of identifications.

However, biological anthropologists once again have a response. They say that this type of classification, yes, is practically useful for crime identification, but beyond that, it has very limited use. If forensic anthropologists want to help legally, fine; to help identify individuals and help families of crime victims, this is a good thing; but, in fact, the information tells us little that is genuinely interesting or useful about the people involved. So biological anthropologists concede the narrow point about racial factors helping with identification of individuals, but what they want to go ahead and say is that race is not a meaningful cluster. It is not a meaningful way to learn anything about people beyond that low level of individual identification.

I want to tell you about a project that involves biological anthropology and that works with skeletons, but in a way that goes beyond forensic anthropology. The example I will use is the New York African Burial Ground Project. This is headed up by the same biological anthropologist I mentioned earlier, Michael Blakey, a colleague of mine at the College of William and Mary. He works with a large interdisciplinary team of other anthropologists and scientists from other disciplines at this particular site in New York.

These project scientists have analyzed over 400 skeletons that were buried in Manhattan, in the center of the city, during the 17th and 18th centuries. These were enslaved individuals, people from Africa who had been forcibly brought to this country and made to be slaves. This site was rediscovered in the early '90s during construction of a building in Manhattan. I say rediscovered because obviously it was an important place in the time that it was being used, but it had been covered over and forgotten and lost to the world until the 1990s.

I also want to say as a sort of preface that the project scientists quite consciously use the term *enslaved individuals* when they describe who was buried in this cemetery, and it is a descriptor term that I like, because to reduce people to being slaves, to call people slaves, makes them into a sort of reduced type of person. These were individuals who had no choice in coming to this country. They were men and women with lives and histories, and we don't want to refer to them simply and reductively as slaves.

The entire project reflects this emphasis on taking into account the whole individual or the whole population. The project's focus has been to explore the culture and the history of the population, rather than simply going through and saying, "Yes, these people were of African descent." There is interest in the original populations from which these people came, but the questions are deeper, and go further. There's work with both the anatomical data—from looking at the skeletons—and there's recovery of some genetic data that is underway.

In trying to trace back where these people came from, there has been a suggestion that we have many African groups represented in these buried individuals in the cemetery. Some of these names you might know as being culture groups from Africa: the Asante, the Touareg, the Ibo and the Yoruba are all represented in this one cemetery in Manhattan.

Beyond that, there's been work on the demography of who's represented in the cemetery. Fully 21 percent of the burials are infants. There's quite a high amount, and the demographers connected with the project have used this to suggest that there was probably about a 50 percent mortality rate of infants, which may not be unsurprising, as much as it is tragic, given that we know the conditions that went along with this enslaved condition.

An interesting fact emerged in the demographic profile. There was a high representation of individuals between the ages of 15 and 25 in the cemetery, and this is the prime of life. This is the reproductive prime of life, but it is also the time when young adults would probably be told to work more intensively. They would be considered the strongest and most capable individuals. So clearly we

104 ©2002 The Teaching Company.

have a real impact on reproductive success, if the cemetery is representing and over-representing individuals of these ages.

The artifacts that were associated with this population have been studied for cultural links to Africa. The diseases and the traumas that these individuals suffered have been studied to find out about their lives. The important point is that we can find out what happened to them as enslaved individuals, but we can also trace the population and culture history back to their place of origin.

Interestingly, the scientists have worked very closely with what's called the *descendant community* in New York. These are people who would be the present-day relatives, kin of the individuals in the cemetery. This is a commitment that the project has made, to not just dig up these skeletons and work with them without permission from people in the community, without working closely with the ideas and suggestions that people in the community might have.

Michael Blakey has summed up the project in noting its real attraction for the media, and for people who like to read about it and learn about it, by noting that it accomplishes a certain combination of factors. It brings together a vivid contrasting of the human face of slavery, with its dehumanizing condition. In other words, the project recognizes the conditions, but it wants to bring life to the people, to their population, and to their culture.

The kind of take-home point here that I'm working towards is to suggest that this is a much fuller type of analysis that does not depend in any meaningful way on race. We can say, forensically, that we're dealing with people who have African origins, but that it is not very interesting or very informative to stop with that racial identification. What we want to know is much more.

This, by the way, intersects with a modern issue that biological anthropologists deal with frequently and archaeologists deal with frequently. This is the question of Native American burials and Native American skeletons. You may know that there's a big issue about re-burial. What will happen to all of these skeletons that are in museums and labs across the world? Who should have control over these?

The descendant communities in this case, present-day Native Americans, quite understandably want to be involved in what happens to the bones of their ancestors, rather than having control rest in the hands of the biological anthropologists. So all of these issues intersect with some very real-world ethical questions that the African Burial Ground Project is probably at the forefront of dealing with.

In conclusion then, human variation is a fascinating topic, and it is absolutely worthy of study, but race is not the way to go. For the reasons that we have discussed, it does not amount to a concept that means anything biologically, and we need to go beyond it in order to really get to an anthropological understanding of variation. We have begun to talk about some alternative approaches to simply settling for racial markers, and we want to continue and look at some other ways to study modern human variation when we return in the next lecture.

Lecture Twenty
Modern Human Variation

Scope:

Though they reject the idea of human races, biological anthropologists remain very interested in how human populations vary in the modern world. As we saw in the last lecture, it is possible to glean much useful information about human variation by shifting the focus from individual or "racial" traits to analysis of whole populations.

We will consider two types of case studies of human variation. In the first, variation is studied in basic human features according to environmental variables. For instance, evidence suggests that individuals of the early hominid lineage originated in Africa with darkly pigmented skin. Lightening of skin color likely occurred only with the first Out-of-Africa hominid migrations north to areas of less intense sunlight. Variation in body shape has also been naturally selected in predictable and interesting ways.

Second, in working out how humans have adapted to extreme environments—to high altitude, for instance—biological anthropologists weigh the relative contributions of genetic adaptation, acclimatization, and cultural adaptation. We will differentiate and discuss these processes.

Research areas such as these allow biological anthropologists to study modern human variation in vital ways that reflect the human evolutionary past and free this field of study from its past obsession with human races.

Outline

I. Biological anthropologists embrace the study of human variation through study at the population level. We have come full circle back to Lecture Two, in which the population concept was introduced; now we can relate that concept to contemporary human life.

II. Skin color, when linked to the issue of race, is overemphasized in the study of human variation. Yet when approached populationally, skin color provides an excellent example of natural selection at work.

A. One's skin color comes about through the interplay of several biological substances, including the pigment melanin. Melanin acts to absorb ultraviolet (UV) light.

B. Using melanin as a key, we can understand the origins of variation in skin color.

   1. Originating in Africa, the earliest hominids likely had dark skin, to block dangerous levels of UV light. We can see UV light as a selection pressure on early hominid populations.

   2. When *Homo erectus* migrated north out of tropical Africa, this selection pressure for dark skin would have relaxed.

   3. A different selection pressure would have emerged in these northern hominid populations, the need for enough vitamin D, which is synthesized by sunlight striking the skin. A combination of dark skin and little light would have been costly to northern hominids.

C. The maintenance of variation in human skin color is a biocultural phenomenon. Social patterns (of marriage, for example) are as important as biological selection pressures in the present day.

III. Just as human populations differ in predictable ways by skin color, so do they differ by body and limb shape.

A. Populations that inhabit tropical areas tend toward having long, slender bodies and limbs. This body configuration is optimal for heat dissipation.

B. Populations that inhabit colder areas tend toward having short, stocky bodies and limbs. This body configuration is optimal for heat retention.

C. The words "tend toward" in A and B above are chosen with care; not all human populations conform to these expectations.

IV. Some humans live in areas where they must adapt to extreme climates. Study of high altitude, for example, allows biological anthropologists to distinguish separate but closely intertwined processes of human adaptation.

A. Anyone who has traveled to high altitude is likely to recall the biological stresses of this extreme climate. Reduction in available oxygen may cause the new arrival to experience shortness of breath, dizziness, and other symptoms.

B. Anthropologically, high altitude is defined as above 10,000 feet. Human populations that reside at high altitude face significant stressors, including higher rates of miscarriage and infant mortality than at lower elevations.

C. Biological anthropologists have identified several different processes that allow humans to adapt to extreme altitude, in both the long term and short term.

    1. Some populations with thousands of years of cultural history at high altitude appear to have genetic advantages, because their reproductive success seems undiminished by their residence in such extreme climate.

    2. Individuals native to high altitude are born with larger hearts and greater lung capacity than those native to lower elevations. They undergo a type of acclimatization process during maturation, in which they become very efficient at using oxygen in the body.

    3. Immigrants or visitors to high altitude undergo a short-term variant of acclimatization, in which they gradually adapt to altitude stressors, and the unpleasant symptoms felt upon arrival diminish.

    4. Cultural adaptations, such as clothing, shelter, and traditions related to birth practices, may all aid the process of adaptation to high altitude.

V. Human adaptation to extreme heat appears to come somewhat more naturally to our species than does adaptation to extreme altitude.

A. As we have seen, some human populations are characterized by skin color, body shape, and limb shape designed by natural selection for maximal adaptation to the heat of the tropics.

B. All human populations, however, have evolved significant capacity to cope with heat relatively rapidly and efficiently by sweating.

C. Heat adaptations in contemporary *Homo sapiens* reflect our long history as tropical primates.

Essential Reading:
Jurmain et al., *Introduction to Physical Anthropology*, chapter 15, pp. 420–36.

Questions to Consider:
1. How does the fact of our African origins help us understand the phenomenon of human skin color variation?
2. In what ways does individual acclimatization to high altitude differ from the genetic adaptation characteristic of some native populations?

Lecture Twenty—Transcript
Modern Human Variation

In this lecture, we ask the question, "If we are going to reject race as a reasonable way to study human variation, how do we proceed?" What approaches have biological anthropologists used to study variation in modern humans? The answer brings us right back to the concept of the *population*, a term that we introduced back in Lecture Two. We can now relate the concept of the population to contemporary human life.

One way we can start is by talking about skin color. You might think that that's immediately a throwback to talking about race, but that's not the way in which I mean it. Skin color is overemphasized when we talk about human variation as racial clusters; but there should be, and there is, no taboo on studying skin color, as long as we do it at the populational level. In fact, done correctly, a study of skin color provides an excellent example of natural selection at work in human evolutionary history.

First, we need to understand how skin color comes about. There are several biological substances that work together to produce the pigment in one's skin. The key factor that we will focus on is melanin. Melanin is a pigment that acts to absorb ultraviolet light, which is sometimes abbreviated as UV light. Ultraviolet light can be quite dangerous because it can actually cause mutations; and it can, for example, cause mutations that may lead in the future to skin cancer. So what happens is that melanin can act as a filter to ultraviolet light, and melanin is produced right in the skin on the epidermis layer, the epidermal top layer of the skin, so it is synthesized naturally in the human body as a protector against UV light.

Let's apply this concept to human evolutionary history. We know that the earliest hominids originated in Africa, in the tropics. We know that they originated from a common ancestor with great apes. We believe that the earliest hominids likely had dark skin. It's somewhat tricky to know when the fur, the type of body covering that apes today have, would have been lost in the evolutionary line. There's no way to test that, since fur or hair does not fossilize.

At some point, there was a transition from having a great ape type of body covering to having skin as we have now, but in any case, we know that when fur was lost and skin color was evolving, dark skin would have been the ancestral condition because we're talking about the tropics. There would have been a need to block dangerous levels of ultraviolet light. One way to put this is that we can see ultraviolet light as a kind of selection pressure on early hominid populations, and this is one reason why it's so fascinating to figure out where we evolved and then begin to look at the implications of that geographic origin.

We also know that *Homo erectus* evolved and migrated out of tropical areas. Some populations stayed in Africa of course, but others migrated north and went into fairly cold areas, for example, Asia. At this point, the selection pressure for dark skin would have relaxed. In fact, we would get a very different type of selection pressure. Typically, when people think about the *Homo erectus* migration, we do tend to think of it in terms of the temperature gradient—going from a hot area to a cold area—and what impact that might have on body shape and body form, and innovations culturally such as fire and so forth, but we can also think about it as a shift in available light.

The different selection pressure that would have emerged at this point involves the need for enough vitamin D. Vitamin D is synthesized when sunlight strikes the skin, so a combination of dark skin and little sunlight would have been dangerous, and that may be the combination that the very earliest migrants from *Homo erectus* populations in Africa might have had. Why would it have been dangerous? Of course, at that time there were no good alternatives sources to vitamin D. There were not convenient sources you could run to for milk, butter and fish to increase the levels of vitamin D, so you needed to have it by sunlight striking the skin.

In northern areas there's less available sunlight, and what could result from this with darker skin is the diseases or traumas that go along with a decrease in levels of vitamin D. There are, for example, bone deformities that result if one doesn't get enough vitamin D. It's possible that these bone deformities can affect the pelvis, and the pelvis would indicate that reproduction would be involved.

So, if there's a deformity of the pelvis, there could be complications in the birth process, which of course gets us to reproductive success, so this might have been quite serious. What I'm suggesting then, is that the relaxation of selection pressure from the tropics, combined with the need to synthesize vitamin D, would have pushed hominids toward lighter skin color as they went north. So perhaps the origins of skin color can be related to migration.

This leads to another question, though. Why has the great variety in skin color that we see today been maintained, when there are all different kinds of ways to synthesize vitamin D in one's body and diet now, while there are all kinds of mobility in different places in the world? People don't stay where they were born. People don't reflect tropical origins where they're living, and so forth.

We need to keep in mind that the maintenance of diversity of skin color is very much a biocultural phenomenon. Biological origins, surely, but now cultural patterns have to be taken into account. I'm referring to things here such as partner choice in mating and marriage. Remember back to our initial definition of population, that a population tends to be where breeding takes place—not completely, but almost always. So there is a lot going on that maintains the origins, the patterns of skin color that can't be tied to biology but also must admit cultural practice as well.

We know that human variation goes far beyond skin color, and I want to revisit a topic that we briefly discussed earlier having to do with variation in human body shape. This was a topic that we introduced in connection with *Homo erectus* and the Nariokotome Boy, talking about that boy's hypertropical adaptation: long, slender body.

So the two points that I want to remind you of that we learned before are: populations that inhabit tropical areas tend towards having both long, slender bodies and long, slender limbs. This is the optimal shape for heat dissipation. By contrast, populations that inhabit colder areas tend towards having shorter, stockier bodies and shorter, more robust limbs, which is the optimal shape for heat retention.

I was quite careful in those preceding sentences to use the words "tends toward," rather than to say that this is an absolute, 100 percent-fulfilled pattern. Not all human populations can form to these expectations or these predictions. Let me give you one interesting exception. Let's consider the African pygmy populations. These are people of quite short stature who live in the wet, humid tropical rainforests of Africa. We know, in fact, that there are pygmy populations across the world. They are not confined to Africa. We can find others, for example, in the Philippines and in Brazil, but the African pygmies are particularly well known and well studied. They happen to be the shortest population of all of the pygmies, so compared to the so-called typical height for a population, they're much, much shorter.

Why? After all, they're living in the tropics, so how come they do not have long, slender bodies and long, slender limbs? The key here is the wet part that I was talking about, the humid part of the rainforest. If you're dealing with this extra factor, then all bets are off, essentially, about body shape. What you have to be able to do to cool yourself is to sweat, but in a humid environment, if you sweat, the sweat does not evaporate, and therefore it doesn't help you just to be able to sweat, to deal with the heat.

So the short stature is an adaptation to the humidity part. It is energetically efficient to be short and small. It also is true that this body shape gives the largest surface area per body mass possible for getting rid of heat, so we can explain the addition of humidity to the hotness as the factor that implicates the short stature here.

Let's leave the body shape and limb shape example, because we have talked about it before, and get into a new area that involves modern variation according to extreme climate. For a long time, biological anthropologists have studied high altitude populations and have been interested in finding out how populations can manage the stresses that go along with living in such places. Their overarching research question is an attempt to distinguish or disentangle different ways of adaptation: genetic, developmental and cultural. How do all these things intertwine, and how can we tell in a given situation which of those is primary?

I want to start with a kind of personal example. I have visited high altitude areas, as I suspect many of you may have, as well. If you visit a high altitude area, you will notice pretty quickly, for most people, that there are biological stresses. There's a reduction in available oxygen at high altitude, and this may manifest itself upon a person's arrival to high altitude, and some unpleasant symptoms. This may include shortness of breath, a feeling of kind of heaviness in moving around and getting tired. If it gets bad enough, it may include headache, nausea and dizziness.

I'm actually referring to relatively low, high altitudes, if you will; in other words, not the extreme, extreme areas. I lived for a time in Santa Fe, New Mexico. I mentioned in the Language lecture convening a seminar there, and I also lived there for a year. The part of Santa Fe in which I resided was 8000 feet up, which is not extremely high, but even so, I felt some of these symptoms upon arrival, and they fairly soon diminished.

When I held that language origins seminar that I mentioned for you earlier and brought in the nine other scholars, one of those people had quite a time adapting to the altitude. It's very individual, but she was ill enough that she had to rest and some of us had to go and get her some medical attention. So it can be a prominent syndrome at relatively low levels for some people.

Anthropologically however, we define high altitude as 10,000 feet or above, so Santa Fe doesn't even make it for the anthropological study of high altitude. Anthropologists are talking about places like the Andes in South America or the higher reaches of the Rocky Mountains. The Himalayas would also be another example. So what happens there? In some cases, there can be quite life-threatening altitude sickness. This has become well known to popular culture through some highly profiled mountain climbing deaths in recent years.

We have had a lot of attention in the media focused on mountain climbing at, for example, Mt. Everest, and deaths that have occurred could have occurred for different reasons. There may be falls and accidents, bad weather causing problems, or avalanches, but there is a contributing factor of the type of altitude sickness or mountain sickness that I'm talking about. Not only the difficulty in breathing and the dizziness, but this can actually involve real impairment of coordination and a real inability to think clearly—well beyond dizziness—involvement of the brain.

When I was doing some research about high altitude areas, I read that when the base camp for mountain climbing was established for Mt. Everest, there was a really high death rate. One in 50 people going to the base camp died—this was quite a while ago now, historically—whereas now, the death rate is one in 10- to 50,000 people. It's a wide range of statistical reporting, but there are very, very few deaths. What this indicates to us is that, with proper knowledge, these symptoms can be managed, but they cannot be completely eliminated, and we want to talk about what it is about these stresses that causes this type of problem and how human populations have adapted.

What do we mean, specifically, by less available oxygen in the air? It's important to know that this same percentage of oxygen is in the air in high or low altitudes. There's no difference there, but what is different is the atmospheric pressure, so that at high altitude, for every breath that you take, there are fewer oxygen molecules available to take in. As a result of this, the body responds by increasing blood flow to the brain, so it really changes the physiological functioning of the body because of this inability to get enough oxygen.

Some populations who have been living for thousands of years at these high altitudes appear to enjoy a kind of genetic advantage to these extreme stresses, because we know that their reproductive success is not diminished by where they live.

Let me back up just a little bit. In some places, we can document the fact that women who live at high altitude have higher rates of infertility and higher rates of miscarriage than women who live at lower altitudes. That is what we consider a kind of typical, predicted pattern. This isn't too surprising, given the problems with getting enough oxygen.

But there are these exceptional situations with some populations that have a particularly long cultural history of inhabiting high areas, and this difference in reproduction is erased so that high altitude women do not suffer from these problems. Anthropologists think that this is a kind of gene pool response that was gradual, that those people who were able to tolerate the stresses would have differentially contributed to the gene pool, a type of thinking that you are familiar with by now in this course.

It is also interesting to note that individuals who are native to high altitude but who may not have such a long cultural history are still born with larger hearts and greater lung capacity than people who are born lower down the mountain. Again, I'm not speaking of things that happen everywhere without exception, but that there's good data to indicate that this happens in some places.

Let's consider the high-altitude Andes. We know that there are 10 million people living above 10,000 feet in the Andes. This is the major mountain chain that goes from Ecuador through Bolivia to Chile. There's been good work from anthropologists, particularly in Bolivia. It's been noted that Bolivian natives develop larger lungs very early in life compared to low altitude counterparts.

This is a developmental trend, so that in fact, their bodies are primed by the altitude to have a response early in life that's part of maturation that enables them to cope. This is a type of process that we call *acclimatization*. In other words, it is a gradual bodily response. It may be partly genetically controlled, but it is not genetic in the sense that I was talking about before, because it occurs in response to the stressors and develops slowly over life.

I have talked about acclimatization in those individuals who are born in a certain place. What about if we revisit the idea of somebody just immigrating to high altitude, or showing up for a trip, for tourism or work? Recent immigrants or visitors to high altitude also show a type of acclimatization, but it is different. This is not involved in lung formation early in life, but rather, a type of amelioration, if you will, of the symptoms that go with the stressors of high altitude.

So there's a gradual adaptation where one may be able to walk longer after three or four days without shortness of breathing or dizziness. The body simply is adjusting to these stressors. What's interesting about this is that every human being does have this ability to differing levels, but it is not caused by living in any certain area. It's just the human body's flexibility in acclimatizing or adapting.

It is also very true that it's completely reversible. In other words, you leave the high altitude area, and you go back to the way you were before. Let's say two weeks go by or two months go by, and you return to high altitude; there's that need to re-acclimatize. I have discovered, by talking with people who go back and forth between high and low altitude, that it can be quite difficult on the body to constantly readjust, one to the other.

Being good anthropologists, we never want to neglect the cultural adaptations, as well. We know that high altitude populations may take certain cultural precautions against these stressors. For example, if there are situations in which women suffer reduced reproductive success, and that this has been known historically in a population, often there will become a cultural tradition where pregnant women are sent down the mountain to give birth somewhere else.

So let's say they're fairly advanced in their pregnancy, and it's coming time for them to actually labor, this may not be right in the ninth month but earlier. They are sent elsewhere, perhaps to live with relatives, to have a chance to give birth with a lot of available oxygen and also to complete the development of the baby.

There are simpler cultural mechanisms that may be at work: shelter, clothing, or the type of food that one eats. There are certain dietary traditions that increase the ability to cope with stresses. For example, some populations chew cocoa leaves and get certain benefits from doing that. It can be very cold at high altitudes, as well as all the other stresses that we've been talking about, so heat retention is an important part of this, and these can be accomplished in a lot of ways.

So the next time you travel to the Rocky Mountains or some high altitude area, or know someone who does, you might be aware of this process. It's something we can see in ourselves no matter where we were born, but it is also important—and I'll come back to this in a minute—to remember that there are limits to the acclimatization.

The anthropological issue, the research issue that we started out talking about, is how to disentangle these different levels of adaptation; and what this requires is anthropologists who study populations or individuals who move around. It's very helpful to find out what happens when you compare a population who, say, has lived for a thousand years at low altitude but then recently moves to high altitude, versus populations who have lived at low altitude for a thousand years versus high altitude for a thousand years—even better, a longer time period of comparison. So the migration and the movement that we have talked about become factors in terms of time of residence, time of gene pool to adapt, and time for developmental acclimatization to occur.

Basically what biological anthropologists say then, is we want to keep in mind that there are these different levels of response. We have the genetic on the one hand, at the level of the gene pool, which requires time. We have developmental acclimatization, which requires being born somewhere, perhaps not with as long a cultural history. We also have the immediate or near-immediate and temporary acclimatization, and that's available to anyone. Then we have the cultural factors. It takes a lot of work to disentangle these and a lot of experimentation.

We do know that high altitude is not part of our human evolutionary history, as far as we know. In other words, we don't have evidence that there were hominid populations evolving at these very high altitudes. I suppose we could find out otherwise in the future, but that would be a surprise. So when I talk about a long cultural history, I'm talking about fairly recent *Homo sapiens* in the thousands of years.

We're not talking about millions of years of adaptation here, and that is probably part of the reason why there are such limits to our ability to cope, and why individuals do succumb to altitude sickness and mountain sickness. In other words, it is possible to manage this syndrome, but it is not possible to overcome it, and there are elevations at which it is simply impossible to function. There is not an infinite capacity for adaptation.

In fact, human adaptation to extreme heat appears to come somewhat more naturally to our species than does adaptation to extreme altitude, and the very fact that this is studied tells us something about biological anthropologists. There's a whole sort of cadre of biological anthropologists who put themselves into extreme climates to make these sorts of studies; and furthermore, who subject recent immigrants to these extreme climates to test what happens to them. If you want to test hypotheses about long-term genetic adaptation versus short-term acclimatization, you have to get people who are not used to these conditions into these conditions.

So there are all kinds of jokes about the sadistic tendencies of these anthropologists. I have read about experiments where biological anthropologists go to high altitude and immerse people's fingers in ice-cold water for as long as they can stand it and then compare that data to the same type of coldwater immersion at low altitudes.

I read of a study that relates more to heat, which we're getting to now, in which volunteers—and I'm glad they were volunteers—went into a laboratory that was kept quite hot and quite humid, and they were made to step up on high boxes for a long period of time, up and down off the box—rigorous exercise—until they got very tired and very hot, to see what kind of acclimatization response they would have over 10 days. It's not something I would want to do for 10 days.

Getting back to this question of, "Do we adapt more readily to heat?" We've already seen that some human populations are adapted by skin color, body shape and limb shape to the tropics, or for the heat of the tropics, so we have that level that we've already discussed. However, beyond this, we can note that all human populations have evolved significant capacity to cope with heat, and they have evolved to cope relatively rapidly and efficiently, and I think more thoroughly and more completely, than to high altitude.

A key part of this adaptation is sweating, and we know that there can be problems with sweating and evaporation in humid areas; but for the most part, sweating is a very efficient response to heat. If you look at your cat or dog and it's a very, very hot day, you can clearly tell that they are not cooling themselves through sweating. They are having their mouths open, they're panting, and perhaps in some cases, swishing their tails, but in any case, mostly panting. They don't have sweating because they're covered with fur. At the time that we had loss of fur in the human evolutionary line, we presumably evolved sweating. It's a very robust response.

Interestingly, during these experiments that I mentioned where, for example, people are given a work task in a very hot environment, we notice that part of the acclimatization is better recruitment of body areas for sweating. What I mean by this is that there are actually better and less good ways to sweat, something I had never thought about before. Where you sweat on the body can differ, and there are places that it's more efficient to sweat from and places it is less efficient to sweat from. So while everybody sweats immediately, there can be a recruitment of an increasingly efficient sweating pattern, and that happens relatively quickly no matter what population you come from.

I think that this tells us something interesting about our species that makes some sense. We, after all, if you think about it, are tropical in our long-term heritage right back to the origin of primates. We have been talking about tropical and semitropical species back in the beginning, 65 and 55 million years ago, with a primate lineage. We had not completely exclusive tropical origins, but overwhelmingly so, and the history of the more recent monkeys and apes has been the history of the tropics—the common ancestor, as well—and then the division of the lineages from there. So what I'm suggesting is that we are tropical animals, and that our adaptation and the flexibility of our bodies at the populational level reflect this.

I've been talking about extreme climate, and this kind of study that biological anthropologists do is an extremely important part of the field. It's an active, vital area of research, just as much as paleoanthropology or primatology. There are journals and conferences devoted to this type of subject, and I think it's very important.

I also want to press on with a different angle about modern human variation. It's important to understand extreme climate, but probably extreme climate doesn't affect all of us as individuals on a day-to-day basis unless we travel a lot or we have interesting ancestral populational histories. What does tend to affect us in our contemporary lives on a more daily basis is our diet, and there have been some fascinating studies about the history of how diets have shifted over time, and what impacts this shift is having on modern human populations.

It is becoming nearly a truism now to turn on the television and hear about the epidemic of obesity in this country, how fat is a problem for Americans and how our diet is troublesome and problematic. How does all that relate to the way that we evolved? How does access to different foods in the present, compared to our ancestral past, impact the way that we live today? Let's continue with that question in Lecture Twenty-One.

Lecture Twenty-One
Body Fat, Diet, and Obesity

Scope:

Another avenue biological anthropologists may use in studying modern human variation involves comparing and contrasting the adaptations of males and females. Many people would guess that the greatest difference between the sexes is to be found in height or weight. In fact, the single most pronounced feature of sexual dimorphism relates to the distribution of fat on the body.

Sexual dimorphism in fat deposition makes good evolutionary sense. Female fat is typically located in specific areas where it can buffer the body against periodic food shortages. We can understand the evolution of this link between fat and reproductive success by thinking about the conditions of our evolutionary past.

Yet what we see in many countries is not just a predictable pattern of sexually dimorphic fat deposition. We find also a virtual epidemic of obesity among men, women, and children. What has happened here? Examining the evolutionary history of human diet yields some clues. For many people in the world, access to foods that were previously in quite short supply is now rather easy. The human body cannot always cope in a healthy manner with such abundance.

Considering body fat, diet, and obesity in evolutionary perspective illustrates the interplay between biology and culture in modern society. Practical solutions for healthier living may emerge from this consideration.

Outline

I. Modern human variation occurs within as well as between populations. One significant source of such variation is sex; male and female humans show aspects of sexual dimorphism.

   A. *Sexual dimorphism* is defined as differences in physical traits between males and females of the same species.

   B. In humans, compared to many other primates, males and females show minimal sexual dimorphism in height and weight.

C. The way in which sexual dimorphism is most pronounced in humans involves the distribution of body fat.
   1. Body fat tends to cluster around the hips, buttocks, and breasts in females. These are the so-called "reproductive areas" of the female body.
   2. Body fat for males, by contrast, tends to cluster around the stomach.

II. Reasons for the sexually dimorphic nature of fat deposition may be found in the link between fat and reproductive success in human evolutionary history.
   A. Fat acts as a buffer in the human body against reduced caloric intake. Should food become scarce, the body begins to metabolize its fat to prevent malnutrition or starvation.
   B. Food shortages, whether seasonal or periodic, are a likely fact of ancestral hominid life. All humans, until 10,000 years ago, lived off the land (gathering, scavenging, and/or hunting); animal domestication and agriculture developed later in human history.
   C. Hominid females with "fat buffers" in so-called reproductive areas of the body were likely able to withstand caloric reduction during food shortages better than females without such buffers. Fat reserves would have been selected for in this context.

III. The increasing rate of obesity in the United States can be seen as stemming from an ancestral adaptation that has gone seriously awry in our modern environment.
   A. According to figures released by the Centers for Disease Control in 2002, 27% of adults and 15% of children in the United States are obese.
   B. This obesity is evolutionarily recent. In the hominid past, food shortages would have combined with a perennial scarcity of salt, sugar, and fat. It was virtually impossible for anyone to ingest too much of these three substances.
   C. In many parts of the world, access to salt, sugar, and fat is now immediate and easy. Humans may tend to "crave" these substances and find themselves unwilling or unable to limit intake of them.

D. The abundance and easy availability of unhealthy and processed foods is exacerbated by a modern shift from active to sedentary lifestyles.

E. Recent research suggests that the decreases in dietary quality and in activity levels now reach into far corners of the globe. Populations in the South Pacific and Africa provide good examples.

IV. Some anthropologists suggest that a partial return to an ancestral diet may have ameliorative benefits for some modern populations.

    A. Practitioners of a new cottage industry based on *paleonutrition* suggest that modern humans could improve their health by adopting some of the dietary and lifestyle habits of our hominid ancestors.

    B. Some anthropologists embrace (and contribute to) this movement. Others point out that there was too much variation in the hominid past to forge any kind of self-help plan based on a homogeneous conception of how hominids lived.

    C. Whether or not specific pieces of advice are adopted, the field of biological anthropology can increase one's awareness of how modern habits have departed significantly from those that shaped our species.

Essential Reading:

Jurmain et al., *Introduction to Physical Anthropology*, chapter 16.

Somer, *The Origin Diet: How Eating Like Our Stone Age Ancestors Will Maximize Your Health.*

Supplementary Reading:

Consult www.PaleoDiet.com.

Questions to Consider:

1. Why have fat buffers been particularly important for women, more so than for men, throughout human evolution?

2. Do you think that that the notion of an evolutionary predisposition for sugar, fat, and salt could be helpful in selecting a healthy lifestyle in today's world?

Lecture Twenty-One—Transcript
Body Fat, Diet, and Obesity

In this lecture and the next, we bring the evolutionary perspective up close and personal to examine aspects of our own lives in the 21st century, and we'll start that exploration with a consideration of diet and how diet has shifted over human history and prehistory. We can lay the groundwork for this exploration by remembering that modern humans vary within populations as well as between them. Until now, we've been talking mostly about inter-population variation. Now let's consider a little bit of within-population variation.

As we already know, a significant source of this is variation by sex, differences in body form between males and females. We have already defined this as *sexual dimorphism.* If we look in the primate lineage, the quintessential example for a striking way to picture sexual dimorphism is with the gorilla. The adult male gorilla is two times as big as the female. The adult male has a differently shaped head than the female.

We know also that most paleoanthropologists believe that the earliest hominids were fairly sexually dimorphic, for the most part, with a shift point at about the time of *Homo erectus*, when female body size increased, equalizing more closely the sexes, away from a gorilla type of model. In modern humans, we know typically males are a little bit taller and a little bit heavier than females, with lots of exceptions. This is the basic trend, but it is not a very exacerbated difference. In other words, it's relatively slight, considering primates and early hominids; and furthermore, this difference only appears at the time of puberty. Before that—for example, at birth—there's statistically no real difference between male and female modern humans.

When you first hear the term, you might think of sexual dimorphism in terms of height and weight, but a completely different factor turns out to be the most important one for sexual dimorphism in *Homo sapiens*, and that is the distribution of fat on the body: where fat is located in males versus females. In women, body fat tends to cluster in the so-called reproductive areas: around the breasts, the hips and the buttocks.

These are the very same areas we talked about a few lectures ago, when we mentioned the Venus figurines, the portable artwork that was fashioned by early modern humans. We talked about the possibility of there being a type of fertility cult reflected in these small statues, because the faces and the features of these women were completely blurry and under-represented, whereas the fat areas were extremely exacerbated on the statues. Women today may find it especially difficult to lose weight in those particular areas. Even if women diet and exercise and manage to lose weight overall, targeting weight loss in those particular areas can be difficult. It can be a stubborn type of thing.

In contrast, the typical modern male tends to accumulate fat around the stomach. This is what's been nicknamed the *beer belly*. So if you go out and you simply observe a group of humans, and you tend to look at fat patterns with a great deal of variation expected, you will tend to see these different patterns.

We want to ask the reason for such a sexually dimorphic pattern of fat deposition and to look back in the evolutionary past in seeking our answer. By now, you will wholly expect to hear a type of correlation between prehistorical reproductive success and modern-day patterns. You're steeped in thinking this way by now in the course.

Fat acts as a buffer in the body. It's a buffer against food shortage and specifically against reduced caloric intake, so should food become scarce, and if that continues in either an intense way or for a prolonged period of time, the body can begin to metabolize fat and use that as a hedge against malnutrition or starvation. What we can do then is think of thinness as a lack of such a buffer. In our culture, this is an unusual way to think of thinness. We live in a cult of thinness; but here, I'm looking at it from a very different perspective. Thinness is the lack of something important.

Food shortages, whether they would be seasonal or occur on a different pattern not quite so frequently as seasonal, are a likely factor of ancestral hominid life. We know this from a combination of factors. Paleoclimate and paleoecology data indicate this to us. So do the types of models that we have become familiar with, using modern human foragers as referents for the past.

We can review a basic fact that, until approximately 10,000 years ago, all creatures on the hominid line were hunter-gatherers living by hunting, fathering and fishing off the land, without agriculture and without animal domestication. What that meant is they were particularly vulnerable to ecological trauma, to food shortages engendered perhaps by drought or even possibly by competition from other species.

Let's look a little bit at modern foragers as a model for this situation. We know in modern foragers—and I'm talking about various Indian groups in different rainforests, the Kongsan in Africa, and so forth—there tends to be no stockpiling or storage of food. Food is gathered and food is shared, but there is not a resource to draw on in times of trouble. There are strategies of insurance against the failure of having enough food, but the strategies tend to be behavioral and biological in a different sense. By behavioral, I mean that food sharing is extremely important socially for hunter-gatherer groups.

The food sharing occurs at several levels. We know that there tends to be a sexual division of labor in modern foragers in that, to some degree, men tend to get one type of resource and women the other. Sometimes there's cooperation, but often there's a kind of bifurcated pathway there, and then within the family, the two sexes share.

There's a higher level of food sharing though, because food sharing occurs across families, so if one family has a particularly successful hunt or other infusion of resources, there's often sharing down the line to other families. At times, if there's a drought or a shortage of food in a wide area, the entire group may simply pick up and move. Hunter-gatherers tend to live in semi-permanent shelters. They must be able to carry their belongings with them and go when they have to go, and this includes carrying dependent offspring as well as tools and artifacts. So they may distribute themselves differently in relationship to available food by moving to perhaps where relatives may live, or striking out in a new area.

We also know that measurements of hunter-gatherer fat, literally on the body, show a kind of curve with the seasons. In other words, there's often seasonal weight loss. There are oftentimes certain seasons—the dry season—when there simply isn't enough food, even though all these social insurance policies are taken into account. So food sharing is very critical.

I remember when I was in graduate school and we all were told to learn about modern foragers because they're so important for modeling the past. One study that struck me in particular about the

Kongsan in Southern Africa involved the training of children for learning how to share. From the time a small baby can walk, a baby is explicitly guided in sharing, so this is an ethic of the group from the very youngest ages. Children are given beads, for example, or other small objects or food, and they're kind of gently pushed over to another adult, told to open their hand and rewarded for food sharing.

All of this indicates that food shortages and periodic weight loss are a problem perennially across the globe for modern human gatherers and hunters, and we want to then use that as our model for the past. What we're suggesting in this lecture is that there well may have been such social insurance policies as we've just talked about with food sharing and moving, but also there might have been a real selection pressure for biological buffers, i.e. fat stores.

In other words, hominid females who had fat in these reproductive areas that the body could metabolize would have had a hedge against these periodic caloric reductions; and the key point is differential reproductive success, that those hominid females with such fat would have done better in terms of producing healthy offspring than hominids without.

Why, really, is fat so important for females? It's probably obvious to you by now, but I do want to talk a little bit more about the reason, which has to do with carrying a child, and particularly lactation, nursing a child, the great energy-related expense of these processes, which affect women rather than men. Again, we are going to rely on models in the present day to infer something about nursing in the hominid past, and here the data from primatology and paleoanthropology nicely converge.

Both the great apes—chimps, gorillas, orangutans, bonobos—and modern foragers tend to nurse infants for the same period of time: three or four years. There's a very robust pattern and statistic that emerges. This is very interesting. This is a long time, and I'm not talking about just the occasional nursing bout, either. The type of nursing that goes on in these creatures is around the clock, 24 hours, and on demand, so the infant tends to be in control. When the infant wants to nurse, day or night, the mother is responsive. Of course, this may change in the third and fourth year. It may not be quite so much on demand, but in any case, it very much is in the beginning years.

We can see how much energy and how many calories would be required to sustain this type of behavior, and how dangerous it would be not to have a buffer in case of trouble. I'm often struck by the difference in nursing today in the modern world as contrasted with what appears to be a very evolutionarily robust pattern of three and four years of nursing. I'm sure we all know women who have breast-fed their babies, but I doubt there are very many of us who know women who breast-fed on demand, around the clock for two years, much less three or four.

Certainly I include myself in the category of women who did not do that. I was able to breast-feed my daughter, but not on that schedule; and this is because the modern world has simply different constraints. Many women work. Many women have less support for child care. There are not extended families. But it's just an interesting sort of comparison that we can keep in mind when we think about nursing in the past.

So what am I really saying about hominids? I'm not trying to claim that hominid women were obese or fat, clearly not. This would not have worked with their active lifestyle and all the food shortages that I've been implying here. What I am suggesting is that some access to bodily fat in the reproductive areas of the body would have been beneficial.

Now we can take our shift to the modern day, and the central claim that I'm making, following other biological anthropologists, is that the increasing rate of obesity we see today in the United States and elsewhere is the manifestation of this ancestral adaptation that has essentially gone out of control, with something that was adaptive in our ancestral environment no longer being so because of changing conditions.

Let me give you some statistics that have been released in 2002 by the Centers for Disease Control, the CDC, in Atlanta. These relate to the United States. According to these data, 27 percent of adults in this country are obese today. That is over a quarter of us in this country. The figure for children is equally, if not more alarming: 15 percent of children are clinically obese. So we're beyond just a little overweight here. We're talking about obesity.

I want to stick in a kind of comment, because I have been following these numbers and the play in the media around them, and already, even though those statistics are quite new, there's a backlash to them. The reason there's a backlash is that it turns out that these statistics are based on pure poundage and height. You give your height, you give your weight, and then it's decided whether or not you're obese. So even if you're extremely fit and well muscled, but you have a lot of body mass, you can still be classified as obese if your pounds are high for your height. There was a kind of sarcastic media story about how a lot of very fit athletes would be considered obese on this measurement system, and Arnold Schwarzenegger would be considered obese on this system. So there may need to be a little bit of tweaking of the measurement system.

But I also know that other studies in the U.S. and elsewhere have all come up with the same trend, and I actually have a lot of confidence in these figures. I think we do have a problem, and it's not only the obesity per se but the danger to health that this indicates via, for example, cardiovascular disease, diabetes, and so forth. So the obesity in our terms is evolutionarily recent and increasing.

We already talked about food shortages that were periodic in the hominid past, but we also need to point out another factor, that there would have been perennial shortage of three critical substances: fat, sugar and salt. From all the evidence that we have at our fingertips as biological anthropologists, we know that there could not have been an abundance or an excess of any of these three critical elements in the past. Yes, there was some fat available through hunting, but not very much. Yes, there's some fruit that has sugar, and there may be small sources of salt, but the point for our purposes is that it would have been ancestrally, for hominids, virtually impossible to ingest too much of these substances.

Of course, the situation is different today, and dramatically different in many parts of the globe, although not all. In many parts of the world, we have quite easy access to sugar, to salt and to fat; and in some cases, humans may find themselves literally craving these substances. In the past, if there were such a desire to eat these substances whenever they would have been found, that would have turned out quite OK because there weren't so much of them. Now, with easy abundance, if there is either an unwillingness or inability to moderate our intake of these, problems can result.

I have often joked with my students about my own addiction to chocolate. This is the one substance in the world that I find hard to resist, and I've often wondered if I am not just showing my well-adaptedness, if you will. I was preparing this morning, going over my notes for this lecture, and I had the TV on in the background, and at one particular news story, my head snapped up with attention. There's a department store in London some of you may have heard of called Fortnum & Mason's—very famous—and right now the department store is seeking a chocolate taster to fly around the world, to sample gourmet chocolate and to report back. My attention was caught by this story. So if I ever give up anthropology, I know where I'm applying.

But the situation really isn't so funny because of the link that I mentioned earlier between the obesity that can result from such types of food desires that we feel, the abundance that is out there of these elements in the world, and the disease. Again, I mention heart disease and diabetes, particularly.

I was reading the *New York Times* the other day, and I read a phrase that struck my attention. It referred to the *cornified* food system in the United States, the great dependence we in this country have on corn and corn products. I was reading this because of my interest in the evolution of diet, and I thought, "That actually sounds quite healthy. How bad could corn be?" Then I realized that the thrust of this particular essay had to do with high fructose corn syrup.

In fact, most snack companies and cola and soda companies in this country no longer use sugar, but they use high fructose corn syrup. It is much cheaper than using sugar, and it is not very healthy. One study suggests that the typical American adult ingest fully 10 percent of his or her calories through corn syrup in all the products that we eat, without even necessarily realizing it. This is another example of a really refined and processed food that tends to appear in the items in our diet, possibly without our even realizing it.

This type of situation is only exacerbated by a shift away from a very active lifestyle to, for many of us, a more sedentary lifestyle. Many of us exercise and work out, but on the whole, over time—and again, we're talking evolutionarily here, the long sweep of time—there has been a decrease in physical activity. Many of us work at desks and commute via cars or trains or subway cars. We're not necessarily walking to work and bicycling to work, or walking out in the world every single day, as people did in the hominid past, so we don't want to forget that aspect that contributes in a dynamic way with the changes in diet.

Until quite recently, I used to teach that this phenomenon of dietary shift—and also we could add in the exercise sedentary shift—was pretty much an artifact of developed countries, urban/suburban environments, the type of countries like the United States, and that the rest of the world was still protected from all of this to some degree. It turns out that I was wrong, and recent data underscore the inaccuracy of that particular view.

For example, populations in the South Pacific and Africa are showing similarly increased obesity levels. I can give you one specific example that emerged from the annual meeting of anthropologists recently that relates to the South Pacific. The Cook Islands in the South Pacific was the locus for this study, and men were measured for obesity levels. In the year 1996, fully 52 percent of men were measured as clinically obese. Compared to 30 years earlier, 1966, only 14 percent of men were obese.

This is a rapid and alarming change in a short period of time, and it doesn't bode well, especially because it's coupled with similar data sets from other societies in undeveloped countries around the world. So we need to start to think of this as more of a global trend, rather than simply a developed country, Western Europe and United States type of trend.

Some anthropologists suggest, in wanting to help out with this situation, that a partial return to our ancestral diet may be useful, that it might help some modern populations or modern individuals. In fact, there's what we can think of as a new cottage industry that emerges from this concern. I've spoken with you before about how biological anthropologists want to be of practical use in the world rather than simply academic theorists. This emerging cottage industry can take the term *paleonutrition studies*, the idea that if we look back at what happened in the past and emulate some of the dietary choices that our ancestors made, perhaps we can in some way improve our health.

There is a wide range of paleonutrition type of self-help guides, books, journal articles, TV essays and stories out there, and they are probably what you would expect. Some of them are more sensational, kind of trading on the idea of, "let's return to our past," whereas others are much more scientific, with more data. Some of them converge on conclusions that are really common sense conclusions: to avoid high levels of processed, refined food and high levels of sugar, salt and fat. Some of them get more specific, and they can be both quite fun and informative.

One book that I read compared what it's like to go to McDonald's and get a quarter-pounder to having eaten in the past a quarter pound of relatively lean meat, such as might have been gained from hominid hunting. There's a certain amount of speculation here, but it's possible, through experimental archaeology and other things, to actually bring down the carcass of an animal, hunt something or scavenge something from an animal that has died, using Oldowan-type tools. Experimental archaeologists do this all the time to try to replicate what might have happened in the past.

So if you get a quarter pound of meat from something like a modern day animal that might have stood in for some prey in the past, you can compare the sort of chemical or nutritional composition of that piece of meat to what you find when you lay your money down at the McDonald's counter and you say, "Quarter-pounder, please." There's an enormous difference in fat level, in salt level, in potassium level and all of these other things, so that we can get a sense of just how much our diet has shifted.

Of course, when we go to fast-food places—and I don't mean to pick on them; this can happen in our own homes—Americans tend to think now in terms of super-sizes. There's "Biggie" fries. There's "Biggie" drinks. There are enormous amounts of things, and so we're used to a whole different societal context now than we had in the past, and these books make that very, very clear. So some anthropologists have been co-authors or co-producers of such attempts.

However, other anthropologists remain quite skeptical of such attempts and feel that they may be harmful, or at the very least, not helpful to dealing with medical problems that relate to our increasing obesity levels. For example, the real worry is that what these paleonutrition people are suggesting is that there was a type of single diet in the hominid past, that we can somehow look back and say, "This is what hominids did," as if there was a homogeneous environment and a homogeneous response.

This is the first of two problems that some biological anthropologist have; in other words, it's a problem we've come up against time and time again: essentializing, making things too simple, saying that things were a certain way, when in fact, we know that there would have been a lot of different environments in which hominids lived, a lot of different dietary patterns, depending on where the group was living.

The second concern biological anthropologists express has to do with the fact that this tends to romanticize the past—the kind of "noble savage" idea, if you will—that hominids were all in tune with their environment, and they instinctively knew what to do, and they just ate so well, and modern times are just completely out of whack, and everything is wrong today, and we can better ourselves by going back into the past. This is surely simplistic.

I can give you an example that I think speaks to both of these concerns in different ways, and the example has to do with lactose intolerance. Lactose is a sugar that's found in dairy products such as milk and ice cream, and some people find lactose intolerance results when they drink milk or have a lot of cheese, yogurt and ice cream. Lactose intolerance can result in some pretty unpleasant symptoms: diarrhea and other digestive upsets. This has been a concern to a lot of people.

However, if you look at this from an evolutionary perspective, lactose intolerance is actually the general condition of mammals. All mammals, by definition, are adapted to drink milk as infants. This is their source of nutrition, mother's milk. They have an enzyme that allows them to easily process the milk, but typically in mammals ranging from cats and dogs straight on up through other mammals, that enzyme is lost as adolescence is approached, and it is typically quite difficult for adults mammals to process milk. So what we think of as a strange, abnormal syndrome is actually an evolutionary type of platform for the whole mammalian lineage.

It's very interesting to note for our purposes that there were certain populations in relatively recent history—for example, European dairying populations—that really relied very, very heavily on milk, and through an apparent combination of mutation and natural selection, these populations lost the problem of lactose intolerance. Because a lot of these populations were in Western Europe, a lot of people of European descent today do not have lactose intolerance.

If you ask people in the United States who does and who doesn't have lactose intolerance, you can draw sort of populational or cultural history lines back to different origins and different diets in the past. Here, there's clear variation showing up, and it's also pointing up that medical knowledge and technology has been a great help in a condition that has arisen from our past. We now have access to milk, ice cream, dairy products and medicines that help with lactose intolerance. So we neither want to forget about variation nor romanticize our past.

Whether or not specific pieces of advice about how to eat and how to exercise go back to our past—are adopted or not—is undeniable, I believe that the field of biological anthropology can increase one's awareness and understanding of how our modern habits do depart from the way in which we evolved. Simply becoming aware of our habits, and that they might be problematic, can be very important when we reach for french fries, or a very large hamburger, or in my case, that gooey piece of chocolate cake. We might realize that we are departing from the healthy habits of our past, and as in everything else, moderation is the key. In the next lecture, we will continue our discussion of how the evolutionary perspective can illuminate patterns in our everyday lives in the present.

Lecture Twenty-Two
The Body and Mind Evolving

Scope:

We have just explored the idea that the human diet may now be "out of whack" with our evolutionary history. This analysis leads to a larger question: Can 21st-century human wellness, both physical and emotional, really be so heavily influenced by events that occurred thousands, and maybe even millions, of years ago?

In some ways, the answer is a crystal-clear "yes." The underlying claim of this course is, after all, that we can better understand ourselves by looking to our past. To the case we have been building all along, we can add three new data points.

First, we consider the phenomenon of morning sickness found among pregnant women. Now treated as pathology by most physicians, the perspective of evolution suggests that it may, in fact, be a quite adaptive response.

Next, we shift time periods to the more recent history of *Homo sapiens*. Surprising new explanations have been published for why the rate of high blood pressure differs between different populations in the United States.

Finally, we investigate the burgeoning field of evolutionary psychology, which extends evolutionary analysis into the area of human emotions and preferences. A "hot topic" in evolutionary psychology is human mate choice.

Dangers exist, however, in the idea that the selection pressures of our hominid past somehow determine our physical or emotional health. We conclude this lecture by affirming that the human species has evolved with a premium on behavioral plasticity.

Outline

I.   In earlier lectures, we proposed that certain aspects of modern human life can be explained by examining not only culture but also biological pressures from our past. Does this evolutionary influence apply only to skin color, human heat tolerance, and dietary preferences, or might it extend to many more areas of physical and emotional health?

A. Our first step is to see how radically new is this question. As we have seen, acceptance of human biological evolution came slowly (and is still not complete). Using an evolutionary perspective to illuminate human health (of body and mind) is still in its infancy.

B. The term *Darwinian medicine* has been coined to acknowledge the fact that some co-called diseases, syndromes, or symptoms might, in fact, have evolved for adaptive reasons. Fever presents us with a quick introductory example.

II. The phenomenon of morning sickness during human pregnancy affords a good opportunity to consider the pros and cons of applying the evolutionary perspective to modern health.

A. As defined by Margie Profet, morning sickness includes feelings of nausea and food aversions, most often during the first trimester.

B. Virtually all women in all cultures experience some degree of morning sickness.

C. Women and their doctors often treat morning sickness as an unpleasant and unnecessary side effect of pregnancy; it sometimes causes concern and alarm among women.

D. Profet points out that the concentration of morning sickness during the first trimester coincides with the period of organ formation in the developing human fetus. Morning sickness may be an adaptive response that has evolved to protect the vulnerable fetus from maternal ingestion of toxins.

E. In our evolutionary past, the foods most available to hominids would likely have included those containing high levels of toxins dangerous to the fetus.

F. Women today who experience a moderate (rather than only slight or very severe) level of morning sickness may be feeling exactly what evolution has designed them to feel to best protect their babies.

III. Health issues may also be studied by focusing on more recent population histories, as is illustrated by new reports on hypertension in the United States.

A. Hypertension, or high blood pressure, exists at higher rates in African-Americans than it does in white Americans in this country.

B. Researchers expected to find that African-Americans ate more salt than their white counterparts, thus accounting, at least in part, for the raised blood pressure. This dietary difference turned out to be absent.

C. Scientists who are tuned in to the evolutionary perspective note some key factors that together might explain the elevated blood pressure.

   1. Many Africans were brought forcibly to this country from West Africa. Their areas of origin are thought to have had unusually little salt available. Peoples' kidneys would, in the distant past, have been selected to be efficient at processing what little salt was available.

   2. Enslaved individuals were forced to endure torturous journeys en route to the Americas. In addition to other stresses, these people endured severe and prolonged thirst. Their kidneys would, thus, have undergone a type of intense "super-selection" for even more efficient uptake and processing of salt.

   3. Under conditions of slavery, this bodily response would have been adaptive. Under current conditions, however, ingesting even typical levels of salt is dangerous because of the "hyperefficient" kidneys that are no longer adaptive.

   4. As with the morning-sickness example, increased awareness of why certain individuals may experience medical problems (here, hypertension) may help patients and physicians alike agree on an effective course of treatment.

IV. The emerging field of evolutionary psychology borrows the principles we have been discussing and applies them to human emotions and choices. The underlying idea is that the evolution of the human mind has been as influenced by our ancestral past as the body, as can be seen through an analysis of human mate choice.

A. Cross-cultural data point to a strong pattern in which human males choose their mates based on different criteria than do human females.

B. Human males tend to select as mates women who are youthful and physically attractive; females tend to use criteria related to status and ability to acquire resources.

C. Some anthropologists suggest that we can use the hominid past to understand this sex difference.

    1. Because women are the ones who bear and nurse offspring, their youth and health are critically important. These qualities are signaled to males by their appearance.

    2. By contrast, the male's critical contribution to reproductive success (after conception) may involve acquisition of resources. Status and power, sometimes correlated with older rather than younger age, may signal to females the male's reproductive ability.

    3. Greater male than female sexual jealousy is predicted from this evolutionary model and appears borne out by the data.

V. Skeptics, both biological anthropologists and others, fear that Darwinian medicine and evolutionary psychology veer too close to biological determinism.

A. The reliance of both these fields on the so-called "environment of evolutionary adaptedness" may be spurious. Very little is known about the social groupings and social behaviors of hominids (at least until Neandertal times and beyond); surely, these varied widely according to local circumstances.

B. The social context, together with learned traditions, plays an enormous role in how symptoms of morning sickness or hypertension are actually experienced and how mate choice unfolds. To lay these patterns at the door of a single set of past selection pressures produces a simplistic picture.

C. We may conclude that the evolutionary perspective has merit when applied to the human body and mind. What we should not do is empower past selection pressures to the exclusion of social learning and flexibility, which are equally key facets of the human evolutionary past.

Essential Reading:

Profet, *Pregnancy Sickness: Using Your Body's Natural Defenses to Protect Your Baby-to-Be*.

Supplementary Reading:

Cosmides et al., *What Is Evolutionary Psychology: Explaining the New Science of the Mind* (forthcoming in spring 2003).

Questions to Consider:

1. What main points support the claim that morning sickness is an evolved mechanism for protection of the human fetus? Can you think of any evidence that detracts from this claim?

2. The concept of variation is central to any understanding, or application, of evolutionary theory. In what ways does evolutionary psychology neglect this critical concept?

Lecture Twenty-Two—Transcript
The Body and Mind Evolving

In earlier lectures, we have proposed that looking, not just at cultural pressures and learned traditions, but also biological selection pressures from our past can illuminate certain aspects of modern human life. Can we push and extend this evolutionary perspective beyond even what we have talked about already? Will it explain other areas of physical and emotional health?

It's good to start out the exploration of this question by appreciating what a radical inquiry it really is. We know that the acceptance of human evolution has come quite slowly and is not yet complete. If we think back to some historical figures that have been mentioned in this course—Charles Darwin, Raymond Dart, and Eugene Dubois— we can remember that all, when they made their discoveries, were met with resistance. Dart discovered australopithecines, Dubois found the first *Homo erectus*, and Charles Darwin gave us a mechanism for evolutionary change, natural selection, and thought it would apply as well to humans. All of these men were met with skepticism from the scientific community.

We also know that even in the modern day, in popular culture there's a great deal of rejection of the idea that modern humans evolved. So it may not be surprising to learn that it is still a very new field to ask about whether health and other aspects of the body, and aspects of the mind and emotions, might be explained on the evolutionary perspective. As with most things, we need to consider this topic in a balanced way, to have caution in how we approach the topic, but also an open mind, with much to be learned from doing so.

The term *Darwinian medicine* is a good example of what I'm talking about. This is a term that's been coined recently in acknowledgement of the fact that some diseases, symptoms or syndromes might have evolved actually for adaptive reasons, that they may be around for some beneficial reason. Fever will provide us with a quick example. We know that in this country, when somebody comes down with a fever, a very typical first response is to run to the medicine cabinet and get the aspirin or the Tylenol, and medicate. This tends to happen—not always, but in a lot of households—at relatively low degrees of fever: 100, 101, and so forth.

There are physicians now—and biological anthropologists as well—who think that we may be medicating too quickly, that after all, fever is a process at work in the body. It is the body's attempt, often successful, to rid itself of infection, so that it is not just a symptom and something that we should get rid of immediately. Of course, common sense needs to be applied. If fever gets up to 103 and 104, we're not going to sit around and be adaptive about it, and these decisions should be made in consultation with a physician, but the very sort of common sense approach would indicate that it might make sense to let fever do its work, unless it reaches dangerous levels. The idea that we're getting at here is that there's an acknowledgement of the adaptive history of fever in our species.

Let's look more closely at a different kind of health issue and explore it more thoroughly. We're going to talk about morning sickness in this context. The phenomenon of morning sickness during human pregnancy is a good opportunity to consider whether the evolutionary perspective works or doesn't work in this particular way. I'm going to rely on the work of the evolutionary scholar Margie Profet and use her definition and her analysis of morning sickness. Profet defines morning sickness in a particular way, to include two clusters of feelings or symptoms. The first is the nausea that women may often feel, not only, but often worse in the morning. Sometimes it happens all day.

The second kind of cluster has to do with food aversions that often women will feel, that food that they routinely had eaten before, that routinely had appealed to them before, is just distasteful in thought. They don't want to get near it. They don't want to eat it. They don't even want to smell it. There are all kinds of pregnancy jokes about food cravings, like the old pickles and ice cream joke that you'll see on old TV sitcoms. Less often discussed are food aversions, but they're really quite common.

In fact, Profet has found in consulting with anthropologists that virtually all women in all cultures feel some degree of morning sickness when it is defined in this particular way, with both clusters of symptoms or feelings. Of course, we can find the occasional woman who will say that neither nausea nor food aversion has ever entered into her experience of pregnancy, but it is mostly a robust phenomenon that is not tied to a particular culture or a particular diet, and that's key to this analysis.

Women and their doctors, at least in this country, often consider morning sickness to be a real nuisance, which it certainly can be, but more to the point, an unnecessary nuisance, something that's just there as a kind of side effect of pregnancy that should be wished away or dealt with. It tends to cause concern and to cause alarm. Sometimes, just as with fever, such concern and alarm is highly justified, particularly if the symptoms are very strong and really incapacitate a woman so that she can't eat, or alternatively, if they're still relatively mild but get prolonged beyond the first trimester, beyond the first three months of a woman's pregnancy. In these cases the doctor and the patient, together, do need to work out a strategy and do need to realize that something has gone astray.

But what we're going to talk about is the mild to moderate morning sickness, which is the typical condition. The heart of Profet's analysis is her pointing out that the concentration of morning sickness during the first trimester coincides with organ formation that is going on in the developing fetus. This is called *organogenesis.* Genesis meaning "start."

When the organs such as the heart, the lungs, the digestive organ, the brain and everything are developing, or starting to develop, this is a time of extreme vulnerability for the human fetus. It is a time when toxins in the diet can very strongly affect healthy development of a developing baby. The fetus is much more vulnerable to toxins. The same level of toxin that an adult could take in and have very little or no affect can be quite dramatically difficult for a fetus to handle.

Despite some maternal filters, this can still be a problem, and so Profet is suggesting that morning sickness may have evolved via natural selection as an adaptive response to protect the developing fetus from ingestion of maternal toxins. In our evolutionary past, the foods that would have been available to hominids broadly and widely are foods that would likely have had such toxins.

We had talked before about how sugar, salt and fat probably would not have been around in much abundance for hominids. What was around? Some meat, lots of plants and tubers; and these tend to be, from what we know of the present day plus paleoecology data, foods that do have toxins in them. So there does seem to be a fit—not imperfect, not really speculative, but it's not 100 percent tight—between the foods that hominids might have eaten and this entire idea.

So the idea now is that women, when they're pregnant, are evolved to be either unable to eat foods that could cause problems for the fetus, or they just don't want to eat them. They can't keep them down, or they don't want to ingest them in the first place. In other words, women today who experience morning sickness in the way I'm describing it—relatively mild to moderate—may be feeling exactly what evolution designed them to feel in order to protect their babies.

Of course, you can conduct for yourself the analysis that's at the heart of this, the reproductive success-based analysis, that women in our developing ancestral past with morning sickness would have produced children who were healthier and more capable of themselves going on to have reproductive success than other women. I don't know by now how many times you've had to hear me say "differential reproductive success," but it continues to be the key concept.

I mentioned in an earlier lecture that when I crave chocolate, I feel well adapted. I learned this theory of Profet's just before I became pregnant, and it really helped. I don't think that it is possible to overestimate the psychological relief that women can feel when they understand that at least there's a strong possibility that their bodies are acting in a beneficial way when they don't feel so well.

I happened to be pregnant in 1993. I attended a biological anthropology conference in Toronto, Canada and remember flying and being very busy and a little bit stressed and not feeling very well, and again, telling myself, "This is a good thing. I understand what is happening." Of course, I want to stress again that this will not work for every woman, that there will be women who do need to understand that the symptoms have gone awry and they really need a lot of medical attention; but it is, I think, a very nice analysis that should lead to more research.

When I teach this in my classes at William and Mary—I teach a Gender and Evolution class—I ask my students to think, "What types of questions does this view cause you to come up with? What would you like to have answered?" We always talk about better data on cross-cultural experience of morning sickness. What specific foods are we talking about that have these toxins? How much do they match up in the present day? The foods that women don't want to eat: are they really dangerous now, or how has that changed over evolutionary time? What about non-human primates? Is there any such thing as morning sickness, and how would we know if there were? So Profet's analysis was a starting point, and other scholars have taken it up and continue to write about it and continue to investigate it.

Health issues may also be studied with looking at more recent population histories rather than going back quite as far as the hominid past. We will consider this by discussing the phenomenon of hypertension in the United States. Hypertension, as you'll know, is just another term for high blood pressure, and recent medical analysis has found that there are higher rates of high blood pressure in African-Americans in this country than in their white counterparts.

We want to be careful here because it sounds very much like we're reverting to the very type of racially based analysis that we rejected several lectures ago, so I want to say a word about that. First of all, when I'm reporting medical data, I do need to use the categories that the physicians and the researchers have used, and we know that racial categories are quite common in such reporting, as they are in the police reports and the forensic reports that we talked about before. But the way we can kind of translate that is we should be thinking populationally rather than racially, and we can realize that there are going to be overlaps between groups and that we're not making claims of genetic isolation or pure groups in any sense.

The medical researchers expected to find that African-Americans ate more salt and that this was at least in part contributing to their higher levels of blood pressure—because we do know that salt has been implicated in blood pressure problems. However, this dietary difference that had been hypothesized turned out to be absent when the diets of the two different populations were studied.

This was a very good time for evolutionary scientists to come in and to look at the problem, and there has been a very interesting publication on this topic that I think might help to account in part for the difference in high blood pressure. I want to stress that I'm not suggesting that this could be the entire answer but rather a contributory factor, and it's again one of those things that is so new that it will require more research.

Many Africans, as we are well aware, were brought forcibly to this country from West Africa. I'm talking here about enslaved individuals. We discussed this population in an earlier lecture, as well. Some people who have studied paleoclimate have noticed that at least some of the areas of origin in West Africa from which these people were taken and brought here seem to have very little salt available in the past. This is not all that surprising. We've talked before about how in natural environments in the past, there doesn't tend to be a lot of salt anyway, but in these areas of West Africa, as far as people can tell, there seems to be a little bit unusual reduction in available salt.

What this would set up then, is a kind of selection pressure for people living in this area generally to have pretty efficient kidneys. In other words, to process the salt that was in the environment in an efficient manner. We can think of this as a relatively mild selection pressure. It's nothing drastic, but it could have set in motion a gradual sort of natural selection over time, the type of process we've talked about quite a lot.

There was a second type of factor that might play a role that we can think of in an additive sense, which might have overlaid, if you will, this ancestral condition. This involves the actual journey from West Africa to the United States. We know that enslaved individuals were forced to endure very difficult, torturous journeys across the Atlantic to get here. They suffered many stresses, and among them was prolonged and quite intense thirst.

This is seen as what scientists call an intense selection funnel, a very short but very intense period of time where there's really exaggerated natural selection, so that what might have resulted is a type of super-efficient kidney to really take up and process what is available in the environment. There wasn't much salt and there wasn't much water, so the kidneys responded in a short-term way.

This would have been adaptive in the short term for survival, for dealing with the little salt and the little water that these people were able to get hold of, and then we want to move again to the modern condition, just as we had in the last lecture in talking about sugar, salt and fat, because then over time, people would start to live in an environment in which salt became much more abundant, and these stress conditions were relaxed or released. So under current conditions, with the salt available and the water available, the typical levels that a person could normally, typically ingest and have no medical problem might, in fact, cause a problem.

In other words, to describe this in a kind of informal way, the kidneys might perceive a so-called normal intake of salt in a very different way because of both the ancestral past and the more historical past. So here we have a double sort of analysis, one that's more historical and one that's more prehistorical, talking about selection pressures on a particular population that can explain a modern-day disparity in hypertension levels, and by "can explain," again I mean provisionally and partially, with more testing needed.

As with our morning sickness example, I think that this can be a useful analysis because it gives physicians and their patients, at the very least, a new starting point. Physicians can discuss with such people these conditions and possibly family histories, talk about possible reasons why things might have happened and have a new armament of tools to really try to deal with and fix the problem with medical treatment.

So far, our examples have all tended to cluster around health, physical health, health of the body. What about if we move more to the arena of the mind and emotions? A very new field, even newer than what I've just been talking about, is emerging that is called *evolutionary psychology*. Here, the very same principles are borrowed, but they're applied to the mind and the emotions. The underlying idea is, why not assume that the human mind has been subject to selection pressures, just as has the human body?

What we'll do here is use human mate choice as an example from evolutionary psychology. The evolutionary psychologist David Buss is important in this context. Cross-cultural data that he has collected point to strong patterns in which human males choose a different kind of partner using different characteristics than do human females. He has data from 10,000 individuals from 37 different world cultures to back up his analysis, and what he suggests is that human males tend to choose as partners females who are young and physically attractive, whereas human females tend to choose as mates partners that have power, status and the ability to acquire resources. This was a pretty key finding that went across the world.

I should interject at this point that a lot of the characteristics that both males and females said were important to them were the same. Not everything fell into different groups by males and females. For example, everybody asked, across the board—and I'm talking statistically; most people—said that what was important was a smart, kind, healthy person, partner, somebody who was dependable and somebody who they could love. We often forget to emphasize when there's no sex difference. How many times do you open the newspaper and you read a big headline saying, "New brain study: no sex difference"? You don't read that. You read the things that emphasize male and female differences. So we need to lay that down as a platform.

However, it is still true that age and visible markers of youth and beauty were more important for males, and resource acquisition and power were more important for females. This is something that has become known as a kind of shorthand or an abbreviation among evolutionary psychologists as the "Bill Clinton-Monica Lewinsky Syndrome." You remember the ex-President Bill Clinton and his involvement with the White House intern Monica Lewinsky. Here we have the quintessential powerful male, a sitting President at the time, and a young, youthful intern. This is an example that we can use to kind of encapsulate this phenomenon.

Some anthropologists suggest that we can use the hominid past to understand this kind of sex difference. Let me underline that verb "understand"—not justify. No one is suggesting—or few people are suggesting; I did read one column that suggested this—that this kind of thing, the Bill Clinton phenomenon, is explainable by the past, and therefore it's perfectly justified. This is not the direction we want to go. We want to analyze this scientifically.

Women are the ones who bear and nurse young. We've been over that many times for its implications in evolutionary terms. So their youth and health are critically important, and are signaled to men by their visible appearance, so being young and looking healthy are reproductive markers in this analysis for men, for increasing men's reproductive success.

Men, on the other hand, of course contribute to reproduction, to making babies, clearly, but after the initial contribution, they are not absolutely necessary as caretakers in the same way that women are, because women carry the infants and then lactate. What may be critically important, as we have discussed, is the resources that males may provide. We've talked before about multiple dependent infants in hominid evolution, the need for hominid and later females to have input from resources, and what we are then doing in this analysis is correlating power and status with ability to get resources.

One prediction that follows from this analysis, with just a little bit of intervening logic, is that greater male sexual jealousy would be predicted than female sexual jealousy in the parents. How do we get to that point? We know that when women have babies, it's very obvious who the mother is. You produce a baby, you're the mother.

In theoretical terms, paternity is always in doubt. I'm not making a comment about families or individual behaviors, but I'm speaking only theoretically, that there's always what's called in science *paternity uncertainty*, that no father ever knows perfectly for sure that a child is his, theoretically. This would predict that there would be male control of females, male control of reproduction and sexual jealousy by males towards females in a greater and exacerbated way compared to the reverse.

In trying to find some information about male sexual jealousy in this country in the present, I decided to use, as a kind of proxy variable, domestic violence. So I collected some data using the American Bar Association's statistics for the 1990s on violence in this country, and I want to give you some of this background information. First of all, the most general statistic is that in this country every year, about a million women experience some type of violence—non-lethal violence, we're talking about in this case—from what are called intimates, anybody with whom they have an intimate relationship. So this is very general. It doesn't get specific as to who the intimates are.

Now we can get a little more specific. Of all annual violence against women, intimates commit 28 percent; and when you look at men, intimates commit only five percent of violence against men. So here you have an important sex difference. That's over a quarter of violence committed by people who are very, very close to women.

If we add this to one other factor, we can get someplace, and the other factor is relating to domestic violence. Between 90 and 95 percent of all victims of domestic violence—violence by people you live with—are women, and the picture that's beginning to emerge here is of domestic violence that occurs not only with people that you live with but also at a really higher risk level after there's been a split. In other words, what I'm saying is that domestic violence can be quite high.

We can relate this back to the difference between male and female paternity certainty and maternity certainty, but also, if a woman tries to leave a very bad, domestically violent situation—to leave her batterer—her chance of serious injury or lethal violence goes up 14 times. It is at that point that we become very interested. When a woman tries to break that bond and leave that reproductive context, she's at extreme risk of what I am calling male sexual jealousy, as expressed through violence. So this whole area of mate choice and how it plays out in behavioral terms is also on the rise in research within evolutionary psychology.

Of course, some biological anthropologists are skeptics. Where would we be without anthropological skeptics? They fear that both Darwinian medicine and all of that type of analysis, together with evolutionary psychology, is veering much too close for comfort to biological determinism. In other words, the idea that we can take this too far and, as I alluded to earlier, some of this behavior could possibly be excused or there could be a sense in which it was taken as natural—that being sick is natural or being in a situation in which male sexual jealousy is expressed is natural—and that is a concern.

The reliance of both these fields on a specific hominid past may be spurious, something that I brought up in the last lecture but we need to revisit here. Both Darwinian medicine and evolutionary psychology refer to a particular concept called the *environment of evolutionary adaptedness*. This is so typical a term that we call it EEA, just like we call reproductive success RS, and use this term a lot.

The idea is hominids evolved in a certain type of environment, and we are going to show the effects of having evolved there. By now you can fill in the critique yourself. We really know very little about the social aspects of the EEA. We have to keep in mind the variation in the EEA, the fact that different hominids would have lived in different places. So to lay these patterns at the door of a single set of selection pressures is very simplistic.

Let me return briefly to morning sickness. I had talked about how we need so much more data about morning sickness and its relationship to environmental selection pressures, and I talked about wishing that we had more cross-cultural data on the modern manifestation of morning sickness. Something I do know from work that I have done on menopause is that menopause is also a relatively universal experience for women, not only in the fact that, of course, women everywhere cease their menstrual cycles, but rather that there are some symptoms or unpleasant feelings attached to that. We know that this is not something that's in women's minds but rather is a real, partly biological, partly cultural syndrome.

The reason I say it's partly cultural is because there are interesting cross-cultural differences in how the symptoms are actually felt. In America, there's a much higher incidence of reporting unpleasant symptoms like hot flashes and the like than in a country, say, for example, like Japan. Why this might be the case isn't totally clear. A suggestion has been made that older women have a more respected and active place in Japanese society, as opposed to our really putting youth on a pedestal here in this country, and that this may ease the transition to menopause for Japanese women and ease their experience of symptoms. We don't know.

We may conclude that the evolutionary perspective has merit when applied both to the human body and to the human mind. I have gone through these case studies for you because I think they're quite promising if they are applied with caution, with remembering hominid variation and with certainly avoiding any analysis suggesting that this is the way things were, so this is the way that things should be. We must not empower the past or past selection pressures to the exclusion of what's really fundamentally human: social learning and social flexibility. Biological determinism is such a concern that I am going to devote the next lecture to it, in a different way. We are going to talk about gene determinism, or the lack of gene determinism, in the next lecture.

Lecture Twenty-Three
Tyranny of the Gene?

Scope:

We have just emphasized human social learning and flexibility as twin pillars of the human evolutionary legacy. Yet, in academic and popular science, many of the latest "hot topics" revolve not around the interplay of biology and culture but around the role of genes in determining human behavior and health.

Americans are currently bombarded with news stories about discoveries related to sequencing the human genome, the potential for gene therapies in conquering various diseases, and the volatile issue of cloning. We are even invited to consider cloning our pets! Analysis of pet cloning serves to show how dangerously oversimplified "gene discourse" has become—and how this oversimplification may affect the way we think about our own lives.

Despite the promise of genetic "quick fixes," the truth is that genes are just one part of a complex interrelated system. Genes do not determine appearance or health, let alone behavior. Discourse implying that genes will unlock new secrets of human health and happiness in the next century deserves skeptical analysis.

Outline

I. In the words of the philosopher of science Evelyn Fox Keller, "never in the history of the gene has the term had more prominence."

   A. We live now in an era that looks to the gene not only as a major explanatory factor in aspects of present-day health and behavior but also as a vehicle to improve health and behavior in the future.

   B. The media find enormously "sexy" such topics as sequencing the human genome, genetic therapies for human diseases, and the ethics of cloning. The power of the gene is virtually taken for granted in these presentations: If genetic problems exist, modern science can fix them by understanding and working with the gene.

C. An accurate scientific picture of the gene clarifies that only very rarely is there a 1:1 relationship between a gene and a specific outcome (whether physical or behavioral). Even a 1:1 relationship between a gene and the production of a specific protein is unusual.

II. A good place to start in exploring these topics is pet cloning.

   A. Among the animals that have now been successfully cloned is the domestic cat; this feat was front-page news in 2002.

   B. Biotechnology companies now advertise widely available cat cloning as a coming reality; they invite customers to freeze their pets' tissue samples for future genetic duplication.

   C. Although the fine print in these advertisements does refer to "slight differences," including those in appearance, between donor animal and resultant clone, the selling point is that people will be able to resume life with a beloved lost pet.

   D. In point of fact, the assumption that cloning produces a near-duplicate creature is seriously flawed. Just as with people, an animal's personality and even its appearance, including such major features as coat color, emerge from a dynamic and unpredictable relationship between genes and the environment.

III. How do the lessons of pet cloning apply to human concerns more directly?

   A. In 2000, the Human Genome Project succeeded in sequencing all the DNA and, thus, identifying all the genes in a "typical human cell." This "cracking of the human genome" was heralded as an enormous breakthrough for humankind.

   1. As the anthropologist Jon Marks has pointed out, "*the* human genome" is a misleading term. Owing to genetic diversity, there is more than one human genome.

   2. Although identifying the DNA sequence in a human cell is indeed impressive, it is not the prize in itself, because it tells us nothing about the function of genes. Genes act not singly but in complex combinations and unpredictable ways.

B. Genetics research may hold out real hope for medical progress in certain areas, but this hope is routinely inflated in the media.

    1. The effect of some diseases may be ameliorated because we understand the genes' role in them. Cystic fibrosis and Tay-Sachs are examples of diseases in which single genes have been implicated.

    2. The vast majority of diseases responsible for human suffering or mortality are not the result of single genes; heart disease, stroke, diabetes, and depression come about for complicated biological and social reasons.

    3. The persistent tendency to think in 1:1 terms may lead to suggested correlations between genes and personality traits ("You may have a gene for shyness; does your spouse have a gene for risk-taking?"). These have no basis in scientific fact.

    4. Just as with pet cloning, the public's expectations in the area of gene therapy have been raised in inaccurate and unrealistic ways.

IV. We return to the words of Evelyn Fox Keller in noting "how large [is] the gap between genetic 'information' and biological meaning…"

  A. Genes should be thought of in two fundamentally different ways.

    1. Genes are structural entities that get passed along from generation to generation and that can be isolated and studied as single elements in the research laboratory.

    2. Genes are functional entities in a very different sense. They have no straightforward functional identity of their own but play a role in dynamic interaction within a larger system.

  B. Improving human life and health does not depend primarily on genetics research. Rather, it requires a solid understanding that the quality of human existence depends on the interaction of many processes, some biological and some social. Biological anthropology provides a window into this complex understanding.

Essential Reading:

Keller, *The Century of the Gene*.

Marks, *What It Means to Be 98% Chimpanzee*, chapter 9.

Questions to Consider:

1. Why do you think the media, and some factions of the public, are so quick to embrace "gene discourse"?

2. What does it mean to say that genes have no functional identity of their own?

Lecture Twenty-Three—Transcript
Tyranny of the Gene?

In this penultimate lecture we return to a micro-level focus. By this I mean, we return to a consideration of the gene. We'll be contrasting the anthropological tendency to take a biocultural look at modern behavior and health with the very popular tendency to give power to the gene and suggest that the gene can determine health and behavior. In the words of Evelyn Fox Keller, who's a prominent philosopher of science, "Never in the history of the term 'gene' has that word had more prominence." I always recommend Keller's books. She is a philosopher of science at MIT. In the written material for this course, I have suggested reading her *Century of the Gene*, and some of what I say in this lecture will be taken from her book.

It is not an overstatement to say that we live in an era that looks to the gene as both an explanatory factor in health and behavior, and as a possible vehicle to fixing problems. I refer here to problems such as with diseases, with health, and also with emotions and things like anxiety and shyness. I have noticed a great simplifying tendency in the media in talking about this topic that I think raises public expectations in the ways that I've just talked about.

For example, the trailer for a TV documentary or the headline of an article is often reductionistic and quite sensationalistic, and tends to focus on gene power, even if the documentary itself or the article itself ends up talking in much more subtle terms and more interactive terms about how a gene may interact with the environment. Further, I find that the media tends to consider quite sexy these so-called "power of the gene" topics; for example, genetic counseling, possible genetic therapy for diseases, the human genome work that's been going on that we'll talk about in a little while, and certainly cloning. Cloning has been very much in the news.

In many of these presentations, there is a certain power that's afforded to the gene that stands in stark contrast to the perspective that we've been developing. The perspective we've talked about has always been one of balance in talking about biology and culture, and also in talking about the gene itself as part of a larger system. So we are going to work on contrasting these perspectives in this lecture.

To remind you of some of the things that we mentioned way back in Lecture Two, an accurate scientific picture of the gene reminds us that only very rarely is there a one-to-one relationship between a gene and some behavioral outcome. It is even true to say that there's not often a one-to-one relationship between the work of a specific, single gene and the production of a specific, single protein.

We know that multiple genes may work together to produce an effect. We know also that a single gene can be affected in many ways by the environment, and we know that there are whole areas on the human genome, on the chromosomes, on the genes, that don't work to produce proteins, that are so-called non-coding regions. So it is with this information that we look back to Lecture Two, which we want to import here in Lecture Twenty-Three.

A good place to start our consideration of these topics is with the phenomenon of pet cloning. Among the animals that now have been successfully cloned is the domestic cat. In December 2001, headlines told us that there was a new kitten produced in the world from a genetic donor: cloning. Cloning is genetic duplication. We know that in natural biological processes, twins may result in humans, as in any other species, and twins are genetic clones of each other, genetic clones that were produced naturally, with identical DNA.

When we talk about cloning, we're talking about the parallel process that is carried out artificially in the laboratory, and this is what happened with the production of the kitten named CC, who was produced from the genetic donor called Rainbow. The correct term here when we talk about the adult cat, Rainbow, is genetic donor. It's not that she was really the mother of CC in the traditional biological sense in terms of having been impregnated and giving birth to CC, but rather donated to the laboratory her DNA, with the production of CC.

Before this other species had been cloned successfully. Many of us will remember Dolly the sheep, the first example of an animal clone, and since then, cows, mice, goats and pigs have been cloned as well, but there's something I think particularly intriguing and worth analyzing about the cloning of a domestic cat, since many of us in this country are pet owners and these issues come very close to our lives.

In fact, I wanted to do some research on the Internet about pet cloning, and I found an unexpected aspect of this whole issue that I want to dwell on for a little while. It is the fact that biotechnology companies are now advertising the possibility of widespread commercial cloning of pets in the relatively near future. I want to emphasize that this is not going on yet, but it is being advertised as coming down the pike within a few years.

So if you go on the Internet—or you can find this out other ways as well; I just happened to use the Internet—you can find that there's a prediction. In a few years—it's not specified how many—a regular person will be able to clone a pet for approximately $20,000, and there are even instructions available to you and I now about what to do to freeze tissue samples of pets that may die now, so the technology that is coming, and will be widely available, can be used in a few years.

For example, I was told that if I wanted to clone a cat that had recently died, the first thing I need to do is to keep the body cool, not to freeze it—that's not a good thing to do—but to keep it cool, to get it as soon as possible to the vet so that the vet may take tissue samples, and then to put two tissue samples in sterile saliva and send them to this particular biotechnology company at an undisclosed location—I won't tell you where—in the United States. So there are people presumably—I don't know—responding to this ad and doing this.

There's a lot of information that goes along with these instructions, and included is the admittance that there may be so-called "slight differences" between the genetic donor—which is the dead animal—and the resultant clone, and I refer to these as the *fine print*. These are not made a big deal of in these advertisements, but they are there, and it's fair of me to say that they are there. It even says at one point that there might be a difference in coat color. When this animal is cloned, there may be other differences, as well.

However, my reading of these advertisements is that the real selling point is the ability for a person to be reunited with a lost pet. Let's say your Fluffy, some animal that you've lived with for 15 years, has died, and you really Miss Fluffy, and you are to think ahead of the possibility of being reunited with a clone of Fluffy. This strikes very close to some of us. I have had cats. I've lived with cats my whole life. My husband and I in the last couple of years lost two cats to cancer, and we miss them very much, so I think that there is a sort of emotional tug when we hear about the possibility that there could be this type of cloning.

To anyone who might consider this, I would recommend trying to find photographs of CC and Rainbow and putting them side-by-side. This is possible with an Internet search. When you put the photos side by side, you'll be struck, I believe, by the really big differences in physical appearance between the two. Even though this is cloning and genetic duplication, the two cats, even over and above the fact that one's a kitten, look different. Their coat patterns are different. Their coat color is different. Many people do not really expect this. This goes to show that genes do not directly control expression of even something as physical and concrete as coat color.

What about what else makes a cat special? Certainly, we become attached to our pets for reasons other than coat color. There may be specific playing games that happen between you and your cat, specific affectionate routines that you might have, and these are not under genetic control, and you don't end up with a cat that is just like the cat that you lost. So in point of fact, there are assumptions behind cloning that are seriously flawed. There are assumptions that cloning is going to end up with either a duplicate or a near-duplicate creature, and the point that I'm making here is that this is not true with appearance, and it is not true with personality and temperament, either.

When I was doing all of this reading, I decided to consult the HSUS, the Humane Society of the United States. This is a group of people I admire. They're a kind of animal protection league. They're very interested in helping animals around the country and helping people help animals. They have a specific response to the entire possibility of widespread commercial pet cloning posted on an Internet site, and they mail this out, as well, to people who are interested. They make three points that I think dovetail very nicely with what I am saying as well.

First, they point out that medical complications seem to go along with cloning. From the other animals that we know about—the sheep, the cows, the pigs and so on—there is what I can call a trend or at least a red flag that there may be health problems and weakness, medical problems associated with cloning. Cloning is very new. We don't have many animals around who have lived a long life and have themselves reproduced successfully, healthfully, so there is this possibility that we need to keep an eye on. We don't know how cloned animals will do.

Secondly, the HSUS underscores the fact that the unique features of an animal cannot be cloned, something we have already reviewed. Thirdly, a very important point, I think, which speaks to people's choices, is why not go to a shelter and help out the overpopulation problem with cats and dogs, rather than cloning? That is more of a social point, but one that I think is worth mentioning. So pet cloning concerns me.

How do the lessons of pet cloning apply to humans more directly? If you've listened to the news at all in the last year or two, certainly you've encountered multiple stories about the possibility of human cloning, but the way I want to approach this topic is to talk about the Human Genome Project instead of human cloning directly.

In the year 2000, the Human Genome Project succeeded in sequencing the DNA in one so-called typical human cell. This was a breakthrough that was widely heralded by scientists across the world, and certainly widely reported in the media. The so-called cracking of the human genome was said to be an equivalent breakthrough as landing a man on the moon. This is a project that took 10 years to complete. It was started with specific goals in the year 1990, and it was completed in the year 2000. By the way, it cost $3 billion along the way.

The anthropologist Jon Marks has pointed out that it is really not correct to refer to "*the* human genome," specifically because there's more than one. There's genetic diversity in humans. We have talked about this when we've talked about race, and we've talked about how the genetic diversity that we see tends to occur within rather than between populations. But in any case, there certainly is genetic diversity to be accounted for, and so taking one human cell gives us a map or a sequence of some of the diversity of the human genome. So that's an important clarification right at the start.

More significantly, I would suggest that yes, it's a big breakthrough to get the map of the human genome, but it should be considered a starting point. It is not the prize in itself. We can learn nothing about the function of genes by simply mapping the genes, and this gets back to the underlying theme that I bring up whenever I talk about genes, that genes do not act singly in simplistic ways, but rather in complex ways, as part of a system. So absolutely, the cracking of the human genome is an exciting first step, but it is that.

Genetics research may hold out real hope for helping with human health problems. This is an area that should have optimism associated with it and should have hope, but I also worry that that optimism tends to be exaggerated in the media, or is applied uncritically rather than on a case-by-case basis. In fact, the effects of some terrible and tragic diseases may be ameliorated if we understand better the genetic role in them. Diseases such as cystic fibrosis and Tay-Sachs come to mind here because we know that single genes play an important role in the expression of these diseases.

Let's talk about Tay-Sachs. Tay-Sachs is a genetic disease that is fatal. It progressively destroys the central nervous system, and it does so in children, so that it is very rare for a child with Tay-Sachs to survive beyond the fifth year. This disease occurs in higher incidences in certain populations: for example, among certain populations of European Jews. This is caused by an absence of a particular enzyme, which is in turn controlled by a specific gene. Researchers know the exact location of this gene. It happens to be on human chromosome number 15 out of all our chromosomes.

If a child inherits a single gene from a parent that has this particular feature, that child will be a carrier. In other words, will not have the symptoms or the disease itself, but will be able to pass on that gene that has the tendency embedded in it. If a child gets a double dose, two genes, one from each parent, that child will unfortunately express Tay-Sachs.

However, the vast majority of diseases are not like this. With Tay-Sachs, we may look in the future to genetic counseling, to be able to identify which parents have the gene, which parents are carriers. You don't know that unless there's a medical history that has made you very aware of it, but you wouldn't know, necessarily, if you were a carrier or not.

There's the possibility further in the future of using genetic therapy in some way to help children who do have a double dose of this gene, but in the vast majority of the diseases that Americans cope with or people around the world cope with and die from, we cannot trace a single gene and link it to the disease. Think of heart disease, diabetes, even something that has an emotional basis, such as depression. These diseases come about for complicated reasons, both biological reasons and social reasons—interactive reasons, as I've stressed so many times. Diet makes a difference. Family makes a difference; and some of that is genetic and some of it is social. Stress levels make a difference, and so on.

This persistent tendency that I have described that is in the media and elsewhere, to think in one-to-one terms—gene, specific outcome—may, in fact, lead to correlations that get suggested between genes and personality traits. How many times have you been flipping channels on TV and heard a claim for "Gene for risk-taking? Do you have the gene for risk-taking? Do you like to bungee-jump?" There may be in the grocery store those tabloid newspapers saying, "Gene for shyness," or, "Gene for chocolate." I've always heard that one, as well.

These are tendencies that get reported that also cause me concern, and as usual, I want to focus on a particular example. An example that I'll use has to do with anxiety. This is based on a scientific report made in the journal *Science* just recently, in the year 2002, and I want to describe for your first what study was done, and then tell you a little bit about how it was reported. There will be two parts to this analysis.

Twenty-eight people, volunteers, were used in this study, and first, their brains were scanned in the laboratory. They were scanned when these people were in a particular testing condition. They were looking at images of scary, frightening faces, and the specific area of the brain that was scanned is called the amygdala. The amygdala is the part of the brain that processes fear and highly emotional stimuli.

After the brain scan part of the experiment, the volunteers donated DNA. The DNA was analyzed, and it was found out whether the people had either variant 1 or variant 2 of a particular gene in the body. This is the gene responsible for transport of a certain brain chemical. It's a chemical in the brain that sends messages in the brain. It's called serotonin.

The result of the study was quite interesting. People with one particular variant of this gene tended to have higher brain activation when watching these scary figures. In other words, their brain, their amygdala responded at a higher rate when they looked at these scary pictures, and the conclusion then, was that there might be a biological basis for this brain activation, a genetic basis for the way that the brain responds to emotional stimuli. That's the report of what happened.

I want to add two things that are my own commentary. These are not things that the scientists themselves are unaware of. The scientists remarked upon them too, but I really want to highlight them. First of all, 28 volunteers is a fairly small number to be basing big conclusions on; and secondly, what was measured was only brain activity. There is no measurement of behavior. There's been no measurement of emotional expression. In other words, the experiment stopped after the brain activity was measured. These people were not asked in any way to report emotion or behavior, to react or respond, so there was no such component of the test.

We want to look at how this was reported, and I'm going to go back to my earlier suggestion that often there's a sensationalistic reporting in the media, and sometimes a reductionistic one, by which I mean focus on genes and giving genes power. The article that I choose to read was actually quite good—if you read the whole thing—in terms of including information about what was and what was not done in the test, and it concludes with a strong quote from a scientist talking about the fact that actual emotional expression, how one might deal with fearful stimuli, is complex, that it takes genes, it takes environment, and it takes the whole context into account.

But what was the headline of this particular article? "Worried? Afraid? Could be genetic." What was the first line of the article, or the lead? "Prone to anxiety? It may be in the genes." So you have to read the whole thing. This is kind of equivalent to that fine print I was talking about on the Internet cat cloning sites. Yes, the information is there, but it tends to be presented very simplistically. I'm suggesting, just as with cat cloning, that the public's expectations tend to be raised in inaccurate and unrealistic ways. Certainly, some people read the whole article and then will get the whole point, but there is this tendency that I don't think is necessarily a good one.

So what I would suggest is that I have no desire to be dismissive of this research. It is not that I think we need to avoid doing research on the role of single genes in diseases, or even the role of complex genes in diseases, or emotional reactions, or mental syndromes, or emotional problems, or anything of the sort. I think that it is possible that we will be able to make breakthroughs based on some of this research and in certain targeted ways, to make a difference to the benefit of human beings, and this is an endeavor that biological anthropologists would endorse.

We wish to be practical, and we wish to make a difference in the world, but I think that the cautionary note that biological anthropology is sounding is because of the fact that there tends to be not so much care to take things on a case-to-case basis. So again, we're talking about this over-empowering of the gene, and I have seen this type of analysis applied to many other examples, as well.

At this part of the lecture, I want to return once again to Evelyn Fox Keller because she has noted that there is a large gap between genetic information and biological meaning. Here, she gets right at what I am trying to say. She's hit the nail on the head. For example, let's say we decide, based on some preliminary research, that it might be possible in the future to fix a problem through intervention at the genetic level that can be aided by having a sequence of the genetic string, the human genome; it can be aided by knowing how genes may have an effect on things like Tay-Sachs or cystic fibrosis.

But what it doesn't tell us is the meaning in a larger sense. What else does that gene do in the system in which it plays a role? If we alter what a single gene does by medical intervention, can we predict what effects that will have on the system as a whole? I think this question should be kept in mind.

Following Keller specifically—this book that I've been reading, *Century of the Gene*—we can say that it's important to think of genes in two very different ways. First, genes are structural entities. They get passed along from generation to generation, and they influence physiology, anatomy and behavior. So we can isolate genes. We can treat them as these single entities in the laboratory, and we can sometimes find out their effects on particular parts of a system. But when we map them in sequence, we're at the start of the quest, because we can't always predict how they fit into the bigger system or what we might alter by changing one part of a big system.

Secondly, and quite differently, we need to remember also that genes are functional entities, and here they have no straightforward, easy-to-label identity of their own because they are so involved in dynamic interaction. I just want to remind you of some specific, concrete examples that we have pulled up before to make easily understandable this term of *dynamic interaction*. We started out talking about the fact that I'm tall and that my tallness was affected by the genetic inheritance from my parents, both of whom are tall; but also how that tallness required a certain environment to flower or blossom or to exist, that good medical care and good nutrition were required.

We also talked early on about the disease of sickle-cell anemia, and what we realized is that the mutation that causes sickle-cell anemia, while so tragic for some, is maintained in the gene pool because, in single doses, that very same mutation affords protection against malaria. So here we have a gene that is not just one thing that we can pick out and say, "Look what it's doing with sickle-cell anemia." That's critically important, yes, but there's a much wider context in which that particular genetic action occurs.

We can go on and we can talk about emotional reactions, as well. We need to remember, as I just talked about, that there's a difference between measuring brain reactivity that can be tied to a gene that is responsible for chemical messaging, rather than the actual expression or the behavioral response that comes out when people act. That's much, much harder to study than it is to put somebody in a lab and measure the waves coming out of their brain.

Therefore, we can conclude by suggesting that improving life and health is the challenge before both this whole area of genetics, and biological anthropology. Certainly, genetic study, genetic therapy, genetic counseling and all the other things have quite a lot to contribute, but biological anthropology has something to contribute also. We must remember that the quality of human existence depends on the interaction of many processes. Some are biological, as we've discussed, some are not; some are social, and some are cultural; and it is that window into the social and the cultural, mixed together with the biological, that we need from biological anthropology.

So to put it a slightly different way, I believe that biological anthropology rescues us from simplified gene discourse. It brings back not only the system, in which the gene is embedded, but also the individual human and the population. Over and over, we talk about the population as the relevant unit of study. So I fear, in a way, that this lesson of biological anthropology will be increasingly needed as we move ahead into the future, that the 21st century may be the century of gene discourse; and what I hope is that the biological anthropological discourse is listened to, as well.

I just mentioned the future, and what's left now is not only to just wrap up the course in the final lecture, but to look a little bit about evolution in the future. One of the questions that I'm asked most frequently by students is, "You know something about evolution. How do you predict we'll evolve in the future? Where is the human species going?" I'll start off the next lecture by considering that question.

Lecture Twenty-Four
Evolution and Our Future

Scope:

Is there any truth to the joke that humans are gradually evolving a new physical form, perhaps best termed *Homo sedentarius obesus*? Can we, in fact, predict how human bodies and minds might change and adapt in the future? Might some future speciation event result in the coexistence of multiple hominids on Earth, as once was common?

These questions can be approached with information about our evolutionary past, as can similar ones about how increases in human population may affect the other creatures with which we share this planet. The knowledge gained from biological anthropology, however, can lead us to reflect with deeper understanding on two issues of even greater overarching importance to humanity.

The first issue can be summarized by the term *continuity*. Taking "the long view" of human history allows us to recognize and appreciate our close kinship with other primates, whether living or extinct. We are not just related to these other species in some distant, technical way, as can be represented by comparisons of DNA or on evolutionary timelines. Rather, our continuity with monkeys, apes, and hominids plays out vitally in our everyday lives, in the way we parent and educate our children, in our reliance on problem-solving technology, in the comfort we take in our symbolic rituals and ceremonies, and in our mobile lifestyle.

The second issue can be summarized by the term *dynamic interaction*. We humans live today in dynamic interaction with every other creature on Earth: every animal, plant, and ecosystem; every human across the room, across the street, across the country, and across the planet. What each of us does affects, in contingent and unpredictable ways, what happens elsewhere. That we live in our world dynamically reflects how we have evolved; we are the result of millions of years of dynamic interplay between biology and culture, between genes and social learning.

Outline

I. Science fiction writers love to imagine the evolutionary future of *Homo sapiens*. Will we evolve larger heads to cope with the Information Age? Will our bodies dwindle even as our heads enlarge, because we have become so sedentary?

    A. As a step toward considering our future, let us remember how very young a species we are. We have been a species for perhaps 125,000 years, and the sole hominid for only 30,000 years.

    B. Biological anthropology teaches us that we cannot predict the precise ways in which we will change as our species moves beyond its infancy. Any traits that are naturally selected are those that will allow differential reproductive success in the surrounding environment, yet shifts in that environment are not foreseeable.

        1. The robust australopithecines, now considered "failed" species, nonetheless lived about a million years. This is nearly 10 times as long as we have existed so far. Their apparent dietary "overspecialization" becomes clear only in hindsight.

        2. As the biological anthropologist Chris Stringer points out, the trend in hominid evolution for millions of years was to get heavier-boned and stronger. Only recently did that trend reverse, with selection acting to choose lighter-boned, more gracile creatures. This change was not predictable.

II. Evolutionary scenarios featuring large heads and small bodies, or increasing obesity, are fanciful. More worthy of our effort is recognizing that selection pressures are not a one-way street.

    A. Courses on human evolution place our species squarely at their center. They depict *Homo sapiens* as having evolved because we met certain challenges and adapted to various selection pressures. Less prominent is the idea that we generate selection pressures, as well as cope with them.

    B. Hominids always existed as part of a community of plants and animals, with reciprocal selection pressures at work.

        1. Evidence of this can be seen back in early hominid times when, for example, big cats were predators on human ancestors.

2. Current predators—and selection pressures—on humans include the viruses that cause AIDS and ebola.

C. *Homo sapiens* now exists in unprecedented numbers; there are 6 billion of us. Our actions create selection pressures on an unprecedented scale for the animals and plants with which we share the Earth.
    1. The disappearance now underway of animal life differs in kind from earlier mass extinctions.
    2. Logging by humans in the Amazon and Congo basins allows us to see the processes at work that may lead to more species extinctions in the future.
    3. Social learning and collective activism can still turn around the bleak picture that ecologists paint of future animal extinctions.

III. Humans are simultaneously influenced by their evolutionary past, in the process of adapting to current local conditions, and capable of rapid social learning and cultural change.

A. We are and will remain one species, divided only into populations that undergo a great deal of gene flow.
    1. All populations of *Homo sapiens* are fundamentally equal in the biological sense. Access to resources, including healthy food and good medical care, is not equal across populations of *Homo sapiens.*
    2. Differential stresses across populations will not result in biological speciation. Human mobility and mating between groups occurs at levels unparalleled in history. One estimate suggests that 1 million people cross national borders in an airplane every single day.

B. The simultaneous facts of our biological equality and our constructed social inequality constitute a challenge for humanity. We must not forget what it means that we are a *single species*, linked with each other across populations and living in a community with other species. This knowledge may help reassert priorities and perspective in today's world.

IV. In sum, biological anthropology can help us reflect on two specific issues of supreme importance to humanity.

A. Our relationship with other primates, whether the living monkeys and apes or the extinct hominids, is one of continuity. Please think back on some examples we have reviewed in this course and consider the links with human behavior:

1. Monkey mothers, organized into matrilines, tend to treat their kin preferentially as compared with non-kin.
2. Chimpanzee mothers respond with guidance and teaching when they realize that their offspring or close friends lack knowledge in certain situations.
3. The archaeological record reflects that once early hominids figured out how to modify stone tools, they began to invent more types of tools, each made in more efficient ways. Sometimes progress was slow, but problem solving with technology increased over time.
4. Neandertals no longer discarded or left to the elements the bodies of deceased relatives and friends; rather, they began to bury their dead. At times, the bodies were buried along with objects of apparent value, likely reflecting some degree of ritual and ceremony.
5. From the time period of *Homo erectus* onward, hominids were not content to stay put, near to where they had been born; rather, they traveled and explored new worlds. The Exploration Age might well be considered to have started 2 million years ago!

B. This continuity means that our modern-day behavior is built on the evolutionary legacy of our past. But human evolution has been too dynamic for us to conclude that our current condition is the result of biology or genes.

1. Let's think about what the concept *dynamic* really implies. Change, yes, but what else? Key elements of dynamic interactions are contingency (things might have turned out another way) and unpredictability (the outcome cannot be known at the start).
2. Human evolution has been dynamic in the sense that our biology and our culture cannot be separated out from each other; their relationship is closely intertwined, contingent, and unpredictable. The same goes for the relationship between genes and social learning. Biological anthropology teaches us that we must understand this complexity to fully cope with the challenges of our future.

Questions to Consider:

1. What is meant by the term *reciprocal selection pressures*?

2. In what ways have we humans evolved dynamically? What lessons does this knowledge carry for us as we move into the 21st century?

Lecture Twenty-Four—Transcript
Evolution and Our Future

We've arrived together at the final lecture now. Before we sum up and talk about the evolutionary lessons of our past and present, let's spend a few moments talking about evolution and the future. Science fiction writers, in particular, love to imagine the future of *Homo sapiens*. Maybe we are going to evolve enormous heads to encase our brains that are being so stuffed full with information in the computer age and the Internet age. Maybe our limbs and the rest of our bodies will dwindle away as our heads get bigger and bigger. Maybe we will even become *Homo sedentarius obesus*, which is one of those Latin fictional names that I think Linnaeus, the taxonomist, would have appreciated.

Obviously, biological anthropologists don't subscribe to these fanciful types of theories, but we do have things that we can say about evolution and the future. We can start by reminding ourselves that we *Homo sapiens* are a very young species. We've talked about this before, how we've been around for 125,000 years, how we've been the sole hominid on the earth for 30,000 years.

Of course, at one and the same time as we realize this, we also look around at the creatures with which we share this Earth, and we see some very ancient creatures. When I go to the National Zoo to study gorillas, I pass the giant tortoises and I remind myself that they have been around—the lineage—for millions and millions of years, that the ancestors of those very tortoises coexisted with the dinosaurs, and we know that is true about some insect species and others, as well.

What biological anthropology teaches us might be seen as a kind of negative lesson, if you will, that it's really not possible to predict precise ways in which humans will evolve as our species does move beyond its infancy. We know that any traits that would evolve in the future are those that would be naturally selected for differential reproductive success in our local environment, and that world environment provides us with a key to understanding why we're dealing with an unpredictable future, because we simply can't predict how the environment may change. Shifts in the environment are not foreseeable. We may try to model changes using our understanding and our technology, but it is impossible to know for sure where we're headed.

The anthropologist William Calvin makes a very interesting statement in this regard. He talks about how there's so much concern now about global warming, the fact that the earth's atmosphere may be heating up a few degrees in temperature as a result of human activity—for example, emission of certain gases into the environment—and this is a worthy concern, one that we should pursue and think about. However, Calvin says that in the rush to talk about global warming, most people forget about the possibility of global cooling, and if we look back at our environmental history and prehistory, we see a pattern and a cycle of global cooling happening over and over again.

Furthermore, Calvin says, we're about due. About 11,000 or 12,000 years ago, we went through the last of such a cooling cycle. In the North Atlantic region, temperatures decreased by about eight degrees centigrade, which is quite a lot. You can imagine what would happen if such a thing were to happen today. Really, Calvin is not trying to say, "Yes, there's going to be global cooling and there's not going to be global warming," but he's underlining the fact that we can't predict what will happen definitely.

Let's take some examples from the type of prehistory and paleoanthropology that we've talked about in this course. We know that the robust australopithecines went extinct at about a million years ago. You can recall that these are the creatures with big, powerful jaws and big back teeth. They have a crushing and grinding complex, and they probably were quite specialized on hard, tough foods such as nuts. We believe that they went extinct because they were over-specialized, and they were either out-competed by other hominids or the environment changed, most likely a combination of the two. If the environment changed and these foods were not so available anymore, then their specialization would have been quite a critical problem.

In any case, they went extinct, but it's not as if we can imagine any robust australopithecine or a fictional researcher projected back into the past saying, "Yes, we're on an over-specialized line here, and we're heading towards extinction. We are too involved with crushing and grinding and tough foods." In other words, this isn't something you can see in the present. It becomes clear with hindsight; but when you're in the middle of living and being adapted to whatever local environment there is, this is not a clear process.

Another biological anthropologist has something to say on this score. Chris Stringer has mentioned that the trend for many millions of years in hominid evolution was to get heavier, bigger-boned, thicker-boned, and more robust; and only quite recently did that trend reverse. So if you think of the gracile lineage that we talked about some lectures ago, the gracile australopithecines evolved into *Homo habilis*, and *Homo habilis* likely evolved into *Homo erectus*, and some populations at that time period evolved into Neandertals. What you get over this time is a general trend toward just what Stringer said: heaviness and robusticity.

With *Homo sapiens* that is no longer the case, but this was not foreseeable or predictable. We have already talked about a little bit of the selection pressures and the interaction of tools and the environment that caused this reduction in robusticity. Again, our point is about unpredictability. So evolutionary scenarios that feature big heads and small bodies, or that call us *Homo sedentarius obesus*, are, in fact, fanciful.

What is more worthy of our consideration are efforts that recognize something about selection pressures. We participate in communities of animals and plants, and this community is a hotbed of reciprocal selection pressures, and I'll explain what I mean by this. Courses about human evolution—and certainly I include this one—tend to squarely highlight *Homo sapiens*. Yes, we talk about other primates. Yes, we talk about other hominids. But it leads up to a glorious crowning achievement of *Homo sapiens*, and in this sort of depiction, *Homo sapiens* comes about as a creature that defied challenges, adapted to various selection pressures and coped with selection pressures.

Less often made obvious is the viewpoint that *Homo sapiens* generate selection pressures. This is something we should remember, and this is a discussion that should take place thinking about modern technology, that we generate selection pressures now in the modern day—for example, global warming—because we have invented all types of new things. But we also can think of this in a wider sense, that naturally in our past, before current-day technology, we would have generated selection pressures, as well.

So let's focus on this idea of the hominids as part of a community of plants and animals with reciprocal selection pressures, and I have to credit here the anthropologist Robert Foley. I'm sure others have written and spoken about this too, but he wrote a book that came out in the late 1980s called *Another Unique Species*, and in this book, he really was able to get across to me the idea of a hominid community very effectively.

Let's start with some pressures on hominids. We can see back in fairly early hominid times that hominids were sometimes prey, were eaten by other creatures. We have dismissed the possibility of the australopithecines as being hunters. We don't really accept the idea of hunting as a prime mover in early hominid evolution, as we know. Recent researchers have shown that the early hominids were sometimes eaten by big cats.

Let's take South Africa as an example and go back to about 2.5 million years ago. The hominids that are involved are probably the robust australopithecines, for the most part, and what we find is that through chemical analysis of the fossil teeth of the predators alive at that time period, we can discover that they ate hominids. Remember that we've talked before about how Neandertal teeth can be analyzed chemically to see what they were eating. A similar type of analysis carried out on the predators—for example, hyenas, saber-toothed cats that lived in the past—shows that hominids were lunch or dinner, definitely a selection pressure on hominids.

In the current day, we can identify some viruses as selection pressures on modern human populations. Viruses, after all, are living organisms, and that means that they have evolved to survive and reproduce, that reproductive success can be applied to viruses just as much as to humans as a measure of evolutionary success. I'm thinking here about diseases such as AIDS and Ebola. We know that the HIV virus underlies AIDS, and what these viruses have been selected to do is to invade human hosts and to reproduce. The more that we have encroached on previously fairly pristine environments, the more we have unleashed, if you will, these viruses.

I'm not suggesting that the viruses themselves are recent in origin. They may be quite ancient. They may have lived in animal hosts, animal reservoirs if you will, but the interaction of humans with animals has been increasing as population increases and as we go into forests. Eating of animal flesh, some of these more exotic species such as monkeys and apes, has increased a lot, and there are some very interesting publications that you can seek out that suggest that the HIV virus evolved from a simian type of virus, a monkey or ape type of virus, and that, in fact, there has been a process by which HIV and AIDS jumped to humans and possibly did so through consumption of ape flesh or monkey flesh.

Of course, we know that here with this example, we're beginning to get into the fact that humans generate selection pressures. I've just been talking about killing and eating other animals and encroaching upon other territories. We *Homo sapiens* now live in the earth in unprecedented numbers. There are six billion of us now. Our actions create selection pressures on a scale that must be considered unprecedented in terms of our past.

The disappearance of animal life that's happening on the earth today is not, in my estimation, just a normal turn of the wheel, if you will. It's not just a normal cycle. We know, that extinctions have occurred all along in prehistory and in history, and we can document them and chart them; mass extinctions even, we know this. But humans are—in my view anyway—not just another species in the sense that we now have become so dominant on Earth in the sense of what we do and how we act that the way that our interacting with other species is of a different order.

An example that I can give you involves the way that we interact with the rainforests in the forests of the Amazon in South America and of the Congo in Africa, and I'm referring here to logging. This is an example that I use whenever I have students or an audience to listen to me because I think it's a very important one. Logging causes habitat destruction, and it causes destruction of animal species because so many animal species are actually consumed. This is the part that people don't as often know about.

We know that habitat destruction, knocking down trees, can cause problems for lots of animal populations. Their shelter and their food may be destroyed. What is less well known is what's called the bushmeat trade, the fact that monkey, apes, elephants and other big creatures are killed and eaten. They're killed and eaten because they're used to feed logging crews a lot of times.

As the loggers go into the forest, they destroy the forest as they go, but they're way out away from cities because they're going into this new territory, and these multinational corporations that underlie this logging bring out lots and lots of workers that are fairly poor. They don't have access to a lot of resources, and the logging companies feed them. One way they feed them is through bushmeat, animals living in the forest. So therefore, the animals that I study, gorillas and others like them, become food, and this food gets exported also to other countries and can be used as delicacies in restaurants.

In any case, this type of action which is causing death of animals of all kinds in very high numbers, does not really match the type of actions that have caused low animal numbers or extinctions before; and the apes and others are headed for extinction if something does not change. I would like to believe that social learning and social activism, and the very behavioral flexibility that I have so often talked about as part of our nature, can turn this picture around.

Right now, the predictions are pretty bleak; so when I talk in academic terms about humans generating selection pressures, what this would translate to is animal extinctions and loss of diversity, loss of some of what makes this, such a wonderful world to live in. Awareness is important, but awareness only works if it translates into action. What I'm talking about here is not only that I want to push a particular agenda, but that I want to bring back the biocultural dimension to these selection pressures, that now we are capable of all kinds of reflection and activism as we collectively realize the effects that our 6 billion numbers have on the world.

To give you two quick examples, there's an organization called the Bushmeat Crisis Task Force that's at work trying to deal with these big corporations, and you have to be able to really make a difference at a very high level to begin to work against logging and against bushmeat. We're talking about World Bank level, getting at the economics of the situation. Trying to stop this type of action is very, very complicated because it involves so many countries and so many economic factors.

At a slightly different level, there's a wonderful organization that Jane Goodall has founded, the famous chimpanzee researcher. She calls it Roots and Shoots, and it's targeted at children to understand the diversity in the world and the extinction problems that the animal populations are facing, so children are taught about their actions and the ability to make a difference. This can be quite remarkable when children living in Africa and in the Amazon are included in these programs. In other words, the children are the very people who may be involved in some of this destruction of the environment.

I suppose the message that I am thinking about here is that it is possible for individuals to make a difference, something that Jane Goodall has stressed for so long. Just yesterday, I was reading *The Washington Post*. There was an interview with a young social activist who has worked in another arena, and he said that he made a decision to devote a certain part of his life to a cause that is a very difficult global cause, and he said a normal, rational person might have thought about the social problems in the world today and concluded that individuals really can't make a difference. This young man said, in fact, it is probably correct to say that any given individual can make only a little difference.

He then went on to say, "But I am delighted to make a little difference because, what is the alternative? Making no difference, and that is not acceptable." This speaks very directly to the human brain and the human will, that it can be used in all different ways and need not just be used to generate negative selection pressures. So I want to give a fairly optimistic look here when I talk about reciprocal selection pressures.

The emphasis in this course has been on the fact that there are simultaneous and multiple influences on humans. Our evolutionary past has been an influence on our present. We also adapt ourselves to local conditions, where we live now and what impacts us in our lives, but we are capable also of rapid social and cultural change.

Before we get to the very end conclusions of this course, I want to go through a kind of intermediate level of summing up, and I want to make just a few points. We are now, and we will remain, one species. We are *Homo sapiens*. We are divided into populations that undergo a great deal of gene flow. We know that gene flow has been part of our history for a very long time, but it continues, and probably at unprecedented levels, as well.

We know that all populations of *Homo sapiens* are equal at the biological level, a fundamental level of this discipline. There is social inequality. Access to resources, to medical care, and even just to food is not equal across populations in the world, but there is no way to say that that social inequality can be linked to biological inequality. There is no biological difference that is meaningful in terms of intelligence or adaptation across populations. So to understand social inequality, we have to look elsewhere: not the realm of biology, but the intersection of power, class, gender and that whole different type of analysis.

Further, differential stresses that might result from social inequality across populations will not result in biological speciation. What I'm talking about here is the conclusion that biological anthropologists have reached, a kind of prediction for the future. Normally, we don't predict. Here, we're going to predict that there will not be some new species. Why? This is because human mobility and human interbreeding across populations occur at such great rates, even more so than in the past.

I've continued my strong addiction to reading the *New York Times* and *The Washington Post* to glean these little facts that I can stick into my lectures, and something I learned recently is a current estimate: that every single day, 1 million people cross national borders on an airplane. I found that to be fascinating; and at first, I was skeptical. That sounds like a really high number.

But since coming to this particular location from where I'm speaking to you, I've been hanging out in a park and watching all the planes coming in and out of Dulles Airport outside Washington, D.C., and I can tell you that if you multiply the number of international carriers by all the airports in this country, by all the airports in the world, I believe that that's probably a right number. So I did my own little mathematical test, and it doesn't even count people who just cross state borders. So as you can see, I've been caught up in thinking about this.

Another biological anthropologist—in fact, I think he's an evolutionary scientist; he may not be an anthropologist—suggested recently that the only case in which we would see speciation in the future—a new species, *Homo* whatever—would be if there were colonization of space, if humans went and lived on the moon or another planet. This is because then you'd have very different selection pressures combined with isolation. There might be some travel back and forth, but gene flow and interbreeding would be greatly reduced, and the extent to which those processes were reduced would control whether or not there was speciation. So that's my sort of nod towards science fiction in the future.

The simultaneous facts of our biological equality and our social inequality are a challenge for our species. I think, at least I'm hopeful, that it might be beneficial to really reflect upon the fact that we are a single species. We are linked to each other across populations by our common evolutionary history and by our recent development as a species, as well. So it gives me some hope to think that this knowledge might be able to help reassert priorities and perspective in a world that, on some days at least, can seem very troubled.

We need to spend some minutes really summing up the course as a whole in this final lecture, and I'm going to do this by suggesting that biological anthropology can help us reflect on two specific issues of supreme importance to our species. So, I can give you an indicator of where we're going, I'll sum up these two issues with two phrases. The first is *continuity*, and the second is *dynamic interaction*.

We'll start with continuity. Our data that we have in biological anthropology shows that humans of today have continuity with the non-human primates and with hominids that are now extinct. You can think back on the content of the whole middle section of this course. Think back on particular examples that show that we have inherited a legacy from the past. It is not a deterministic legacy, but it does influence us.

So let's think of some examples that go back over the span of the course. Let's start with monkeys. For example, monkey mothers at Cayo Santiago in Puerto Rico differentially behave towards kin in positive ways. In other words, they act more positively towards kin than towards non-kin. For example, a mother may rush to support a daughter, a sister, or a mother when that other animal gets into trouble or gets into a fight. Even if the mother herself was not threatened in any way or her resources were not threatened, she puts herself in harm's way.

We can think of ways in which we may do this as well with our own relatives, and we can also extend this to an emotional analysis of the way we act with relatives. Perhaps you can think of an example that goes something like this: a person reflecting and saying, "You know, there's a person who was really very nasty to my mother, and although that person never did anything to me, I'm finding it hard to think of that person in positive tones." Someone in your family, a relative, is injured or hurt in some way, emotionally or physically. This clearly has an effect.

Chimpanzee mothers, we know, spend time guiding and instructing their infants. They may facilitate the learning of tool use. They may facilitate proper social behavior, how youngsters should approach a dominant alpha male, and this has immediate resonance for us. Those of us who are parents know that it is a lifelong job, that guidance and instruction cross all kinds of contexts.

If we switch to the paleoanthropological side of things, we can look at other aspects of human prehistory: for example, the modification of stone tools. We know that for 2.5 million years, we have been making stone tools as a human line, that there's been a process—not linear but basically progressive—in which we continue to invent new types of tools and new ways to manufacture tools. Sometimes the progress was slow. There were periods of stasis. Sometimes it speeded up. But there's a clear platform in our evolutionary past for inventing and solving problems via technology.

Let's look to Neandertals for a moment. With this hominid, we had for the first time intentional burial of the dead. At times, the dead were even buried with grave goods, possibly some type of symbolic marker. We're not sure how symbolic; but in any case, it is likely that there was some degree of ritual, if only reflecting respect and emotional ties.

Yes, this is a bit speculative. We don't want to stretch it too far; but I could also ask, how much of a stretch is it to suggest emotion at, say, 100,000 years ago, when we know that there has been socioemotional ties way back in our hominid past, if we can take great apes in the modern day as any example? We've talked about chimpanzees as having theory of mind, as having empathy, and to make this work in the past, we have to use them as stand-ins for animals that were alive before the common ancestor, a very typical approach in biological anthropology.

Finally, a final example: *Homo erectus* as migrants. We know from about 1.8 million years ago, if not even earlier, hominids began to wander the earth. They began to explore other worlds. We could even say that the Age of Exploration started at about two million years ago, when hominids left Africa and went to Asia. So continuity is the first issue.

The second issue is this dynamic interaction, and this is the note on which I'd like to conclude. Human evolution has been far too dynamic for us to give too much weight to biology alone or genes alone, and I want to think a little but about what dynamic really means. Dynamic is a term that calls to mind change. Yes, that's part of it, but even more, contingency and unpredictability are important.

Contingency refers to the fact that things might have turned out another way. They happened a certain way, but they might not have. Unpredictability means that the outcome of some process cannot be known at the start. This is what Stephen Jay Gould talked about when he favored the Out-of-Africa replacement model in suggesting that we evolved in Africa because of a certain combination of selection pressures, but it might have turned out a very different way.

Human evolution has been dynamic in a broader sense, as well. What biological anthropology tells us is that we can't separate our biology and our culture. We can't separate out genes and learning. In each case, the relationship between those processes is contingent and unpredictable, intertwined totally, so that you can't parcel them out and say something is half biology and half culture, or half genetic and half learning. That goes against everything we know, that when you bring these things together, something comes out that is more than the sum of the parts, in an unpredictable manner. Biological anthropology teaches us that we must understand this kind of complexity in order to understand the challenges of our future as well as our history and prehistory in the past.

This brings us to the end of Lecture Twenty-Four. I'd like to conclude by saying how much I've really enjoyed constructing and delivering these lectures. I hope that some of you will decide to pursue reading about biological anthropology. There are many wonderful books, which you know from the written material that you have for this course that I have recommended. There are wonderful journals and magazine articles; and if you do have access to a computer, do check the Internet. Again, I've given you some clues.

I've included in the written material packet my e-mail address. I'm very responsive to e-mail. If you'd like to discuss possible sources to read or Internet sites, or if you have questions, I'd be delighted to hear from you. I'd like to conclude by thanking you and wishing you good fun and good luck with anthropology in the future.

Timeline

Prehistory

(**Note**: Biological anthropologists frequently revise these dates, updating them according to new information. Included here are the current best estimates. The abbreviation *mya* stands for "million years ago.")

70 mya...Age of Dinosaurs nears an end; no primates yet exist

65 mya...Age of Mammals begins; ancestral primates appear

55 mya...Earliest definite primate

55–6 mya.....................................Numerous speciation events produce ancestors to today's prosimians, monkeys, and apes

8–7 mya.......................................Common ancestor to African apes and hominids

approx. 7 mya.............................First hominid, perhaps *Sahelanthropus tchadensis*

4.2 mya..First australopithecines

3.2 mya..Time at which "Lucy" lived (*Australopithecus afarensis*)

2.5 mya..First hominid-modified stone tools

2.4 mya..First hominid in the *Homo* genus, *Homo habilis*

1.9 mya..First *Homo erectus*, in Africa

1.8 mya..Some populations of *Homo erectus* migrate out of Africa to Asia

130,000.......................................First Neandertals

125,000.......................................First *Homo sapiens*

30,000...Disappearance of Neandertals; *Homo sapiens* is the only surviving hominid

History

1856 ....First Neandertal discovery, in Germany

1859 ....Charles Darwin publishes *On the Origin of Species*

1891 ....First *Homo erectus* discovery, in Java

1924 ....Raymond Dart finds first australopithecine, in South Africa

1925 ....Scopes Monkey Trial in Tennessee

1951 ....Sherwood Washburn outlines the new physical anthropology

1960 ....Jane Goodall begins observations of wild chimpanzees

1968 ....Washburn and Lancaster publish "Man the Hunter" paper

1974 ....Don Johanson uncovers "Lucy" in Ethiopia

1978 ....Glyn Isaac publishes theory on *Homo habilis* behavior

1984-1985 ....Discovery of "Nariokotome Boy" (*Homo erectus*) in Kenya

1990s...Excavation of African sites showing that early modern behavior did not originate exclusively in Europe

2002 ....Announcement of the fossil discovery *Sahelanthropus tchadensis* from Chad, currently considered the oldest hominid known to science

Glossary

(**Note**: For names of specific primates, please refer to the Species Sketches section.)

acclimatization: A physiological process of adaptation, as to extreme climate, in either the short or long term.

adaptive radiation: Rapid expansion of new animal forms into new habitats.

anthropoids: One of the two major groupings of primates; the anthropoids are diverse, including all the monkeys, apes, extinct human ancestors, and modern humans.

apes: A subset of anthropoids that tends to be large-bodied and includes humans' closest living relatives.

biological anthropology: The subfield of anthropology that takes as its subject matter the evolution, genetics, and anatomy of, and modern variation within, the human species.

conceptual model: Model that focuses on evolutionary processes rather than specific organisms in trying to understand the behavior of extinct human ancestors.

differential reproductive success: Refers to the fact that within a population, some individuals will produce more healthy offspring than others.

evolution: Change in the genetic structure of a population.

gene: A sequence of DNA that can be passed on to offspring.

gene flow: One of the major mechanisms of evolution; refers to the exchange of genes between populations.

gene pool: All the genes shared by members of a single population.

genetic drift: One of the major mechanisms of evolution; occurs in small populations when random events shift the composition of the gene pool.

gracile: Relatively light-boned and slender.

hominids: Primates, including those that led to modern humans, characterized by bipedalism; evolved after the evolutionary split with the great apes.

homology: A similarity based on shared descent (if two primates have homologous traits, the traits are alike owing to a common evolutionary heritage).

iconic gesture: Gesture that indicates the specific action that the gesturer wishes another animal or person to take.

intelligent design: A set of beliefs predicated on the idea that some organs and organisms, such as humans, are so complex that they could have arisen only by design (not by unguided evolutionary mechanisms).

matriline: A group of related females.

mitochondrial DNA (mtDNA): Inherited only through the maternal line and, thus, changed only via mutation, mtDNA is a possible tool for tracing descent lines in prehistory.

monkeys: A diverse set of anthropoids that are relatively small-bodied, more distantly related to humans than are the apes.

multiregional model: One of two major models for the origins of modern humans; this one suggests that *Homo sapiens* evolved from earlier hominids on three continents at about the same time in response to regional selection pressures.

mutation: One of the major mechanisms of evolution; refers to a change in the structure of DNA within a gene.

natural selection: The single most important mechanism of evolution; refers to the fact that some individuals within any population will be better adapted to their local environment than others, leading to greater reproductive success.

out-of-Africa replacement model: One of two major models for the origins of modern humans; this one suggests that *Homo sapiens* evolved first in Africa, then spread out to other areas and replaced all other hominids.

patriline: A group of related males.

phylogenetic model: Model that proposes taking into account the behavior of all four great apes in trying to understand an extinct human ancestor.

population: Members of a species that share a common gene pool and mate more with one another than with members of other populations.

primates: Division of mammals that includes all prosimians, monkeys, apes, extinct human ancestors, and modern humans.

prosimians: One of the two major groupings of primates; the prosimians evolved first and are relatively specialized.

punctuated equilibrium: The idea that evolution may sometimes proceed in rapid leaps rather than always by small, gradual modifications.

race: A term used to suggest that humans can be sorted into distinct groups based on genetic traits, such as skin color or nose shape. Almost all biological anthropologists agree that this term has no biological validity.

referential model: Model that proposes a 1:1 relationship between the behavior of some living primate and an extinct human ancestor.

robust: Heavy-boned and strong.

scientific creationism: A set of beliefs predicated on the ideas that the Earth is young and humans were created by a supernatural force within the last 10,000 years.

sexual dimorphism: Anatomical differences based on one's sex.

speciation: The process by which new species are formed from existing ones.

species: A grouping of organisms whose members can all interbreed with one another and produce fertile offspring. The species is a larger grouping than the population.

theory: In science, a set of principles that has been supported by observation and testing.

theory of mind: The ability to take into account the mental perspective of another.

Species Sketches

Australopithecus afarensis: A gracile hominid species that includes "Lucy" and lived in Africa from about 3.6 to 3 million years ago.

Australopithecus africanus: The first australopithecine to be discovered, this gracile African form lived from perhaps 3.6 to about 2 million years ago.

Australopithecus anamensis: An African hominid dating to about 4.2 million years ago.

Australopithecus robustus and *Australopithecus boisei*: Two robust hominids that lived in Africa along with gracile forms but eventually went extinct, apparently due to dietary overspecialization.

bonobo: One of the African great apes; lives in bisexual communities with greater emphasis on female-female bonds than is found in the chimpanzees.

chimpanzee: One of the African great apes; lives in bisexual communities with greater emphasis on male dominance than is found in the bonobos.

gelada baboon: An Old World monkey that lives in one-male units; females bond with one another to prevent domination by males.

gorilla: One of the African great apes; lives in either one- or two-male groups.

great apes: Humans' closest living relatives, these large-bodied and large-brained apes are the orangutan, gorilla, chimpanzee, and bonobo.

hamadyras baboon: An Old World monkey that lives in one-male units; males dominate females, harassing and biting them.

Homo erectus: The first hominid to live in Asia as well as Africa, this species, which includes the "Nariokotome Boy," is thought of as a turning point in human evolution. Appearing at about 1.9 million years ago, its "endpoint" is hotly debated but may be about 400,000 years ago.

Homo habilis: The first hominid in our own genus, this species is famous for being the first (as far as we know!) to manufacture stone tools. It lived in Africa from about 2.4 to 1.9 million years ago.

Homo neandertalensis: See **neandertal**, below.

Homo sapiens: Modern humans; us. Modern human anatomy developed at perhaps 125,000 to 100,000 years ago.

Kenyanthropus platyops: Flat-faced hominid of Kenya, discovered by Maeve Leakey, that existed at about 3.5 million years ago. This species thus overlapped in time with *Australopithecus afarensis*.

lesser apes: Small-bodied apes of Asia, including gibbons, that usually live in monogamous pairs.

marmoset: A small New World monkey that lives in extended family groups.

muriqui: A relatively large New World monkey that lives in peaceable social groups largely devoid of relative ranking.

neandertal: Hominid that is likely a separate species from modern humans but overlapped with them in time and place. The Neandertals lived in Asia and Europe from about 130,000 to 30,000 years ago.

orangutan: The only Asian great ape and the least social of all apes.

Orrorin tugenensis: A very old African hominid, dated to about 5.8 million years ago; dethroned by *Sahelanthropus tchadensis* in 2002 as the "oldest known hominid."

rhesus monkey: An Old World monkeys organized into matrilines with great emphasis on dominance hierarchies.

ring-tailed lemur: A group-living African prosimian in which females are routinely dominant to males.

Sahelanthropus tchadensis: Best current candidate for the oldest hominid, at about 7 million years ago; announced in 2002 by scientists working in Chad, central Africa.

savanna baboon: An Old World monkey organized into matrilines and heavily dependent on dominance hierarchies.

slow loris: A nocturnal Asian prosimian that is far more social than expected for such a primate.

transitional hominid species: The catchall term we use to refer to those hominids that lived after ***Homo erectus*** but before ***Homo sapiens***, with a mix of *erectus-sapiens* traits. These hominids are found in Africa, Asia, and Europe.

Bibliography

Essential Reading:

De Waal, Frans. *Tree of Origin: What Primate Behavior Can Tell Us About Human Social Evolution.* Cambridge, MA: Harvard University Press, 2001. This edited collection, with contributed chapters from leading scholars, demonstrates beautifully the ways in which specific studies of monkeys and apes can shed light on our hominid ancestry.

Gould, Stephen Jay. *The Structure of Evolutionary Theory.* Cambridge, MA: The Belknap Press of Harvard University Press, 2002. Published just before his death, this volume is Gould's *magnum opus.* It explains how newer concepts can be integrated with Darwin's insights to produce a comprehensive vision for understanding evolution. At well over 1,000 pages, the volume is formidable, but selected chapters are well worth the effort for the serious student.

Johanson, Don, and Maitland Edey. *Lucy: The Beginnings of Humankind.* New York: Simon and Schuster, 1981. A fact-filled, enjoyable account of Lucy's discovery specifically and theories of human evolution generally, this book gives an excellent feel for what it is like to be a fossil hunter in Ethiopia. It must be read in the context of the course, however; some of its conclusions about Lucy's place in the human family tree have been overturned by newer information.

Jurmain, Robert, Harry Nelson, Lynn Kilgore, and Wenda Trevathan. *Introduction to Physical Anthropology,* 8th edition. Belmont, CA: Wadsworth Publishing, 2000. The text of choice for many biological anthropologists, this book provides vital background information on the topics covered in this course. It includes superb visuals (photographs, charts, diagrams). The chapters cited as essential reading at the end of each lecture are keyed to the 8th edition, but newer editions, when available, would be even better.

Keller, Evelyn Fox. *The Century of the Gene.* Cambridge, MA: Harvard University Press, 2000. Written elegantly and aimed at non-experts, this book examines what genes are and what they are not (and how that understanding has changed as new knowledge accumulates). Keller shows that we cannot understand genes as isolated units, but must instead, study them at work as part of a larger biological system.

King, Barbara J. *The Origins of Language: What Nonhuman Primates Can Tell Us.* Santa Fe, NM: School of American Research Press, 1999. Lecture Eighteen relies heavily on this volume's contribution by Burling, who creates a plausible scenario of the evolution of language from ape gesture. Other chapters are useful for understanding the evolutionary transition from nonhuman primate communication to human language.

Marks, Jonathan. *What It Means to Be 98% Chimpanzee: Apes, People, and Their Genes.* Berkeley, CA: University of California Press, 2002. Marks's title refers to the oft-cited statistic that humans and chimpanzees share 98% of their genes. But what does this really mean? In his typically engaging style, Marks examines not only this question but others related to human "race" and variations that spring from it.

Natural History, April 2002 issue. Two features in this issue explain in clear terms issues of relevance to this course. First is a series of short opinion pieces that together constitute a written debate between evolutionary theorists and intelligent design advocates. Second is the column by science writer Carl Zimmer on evolution of the eye.

Profet, Margie. *Pregnancy Sickness: Using Your Body's Natural Defenses to Protect Your Baby-to-Be.* Cambridge, MA. Perseus, 1997. A readable account of Profet's fascinating theory that pregnancy sickness is a long-ago evolved adaptation to protect the developing fetus.

Scientific American, July 2002 issue. The no-holds-barred title of John Rennie's article says it all; "15 Answers to Creationist Nonsense" refutes myths and misunderstandings related to basic concepts in evolutionary theory.

Somer, Elizabeth. *The Origin Diet: How Eating Like Our Stone Age Ancestors Will Maximize Your Health.* New York: Owl Books, 2002. As a registered dietician, Somer does an intriguing job of suggesting ways in which knowledge of paleonutrition might improve our lives today.

Sykes, Bryan. *The Seven Daughters of Eve: The Science That Reveals Our Genetic Ancestry.* New York: W.W. Norton and Co., 2001. Genetics professor Sykes writes about the uses to which mitochondrial DNA may be put in clarifying issues in human evolution. He tackles controversies, such as how closely related

Neandertals are to modern humans, and gives his perspective on the origins of modern *Homo sapiens*.

Tattersall, Ian. *The Last Neanderthal: The Rise, Success, and Mysterious Extinction of Our Closest Human Relatives*. Boulder, CO. Westview Press, 1999. A paleoanthropology curator at the American Museum of Natural History in New York, Tattersall has written a string of valuable books on human evolution. This one is particularly welcome for its illustrations that wonderfully bring to life the Neandertals.

Weiner, Jonathan. *The Beak of the Finch: A Story of Evolution in Our Time*. New York: Knopf, 1994. Reviewers have noted that this Pulitzer-Prize-winning account reads like a thriller! It details research done by the Grants, a husband-and-wife team of biologists that has carried out modern-day evolutionary studies on the finch populations in the Galapagos Islands—the descendant birds of those studied by Charles Darwin.

Supplementary Reading:

Behe, Michael. *Darwin's Black Box: The Biochemical Challenge to Evolution*. New York: Free Press, 1996. This book, billed by some as "a scientific argument for the existence of God," presents one case for an intelligent design perspective. It can be read as an alternative to the evolutionary thinking that is the foundation for this course.

Blakey, Michael. "Bioarchaeology of the African Diaspora in the Americas: Its Origins and Scope." *Annual Review of Anthropology* 30:387–422, 2001.

Cosmides, Lena, John Tooby, et al. *What Is Evolutionary Psychology: Explaining the New Science of the Mind*. New Haven, CT. Yale University Press (forthcoming in 2003). This book promises to be a lively and lucid account of the principles of the emerging field of evolutionary psychology.

Jolly, Alison. *Lucy's Legacy: Sex and Intelligence in Human Evolution*. Cambridge, MA: Harvard University Press, 1999. An always literate, sometimes amusing analysis of how issues of sex and gender figure into primate behavior and human evolution.

Potts, Richard. *Early Hominid Activities at Olduvai*. Aldine de Gruyter, 1988. The Smithsonian Institution's Potts lays out a fascinating behavioral framework for interpreting the hominid sites at Olduvai Gorge, Tanzania. Particularly enlightened is his alternative formulation to a long-accepted model of *Homo habilis* behavior.

Sapolsky, Robert. *A Primate's Memoir.* New York: Scribner, 2001. An informative and fun account by a distinguished primatologist, MacArthur "genius" award winner, and Teaching Company faculty member. He writes about his many years in Kenya studying wild baboon behavior.

Savage-Rumbaugh, E. S., and R. Lewin. *Kanzi: The Ape at the Brink of the Human Mind.* New York: Wiley, 1994. The accomplishments of the bonobo Kanzi, who can produce and comprehend symbolic utterances, are chronicled in this volume.

Notes